Movement ABCs

An Inclusive Guide to Stimulating Language Development

Jolanda G. Hengstman

Human Kinetics

Library of Congress Cataloging-in-Publication Data

Hengstman, Jolanda G., 1960-
    Movement ABCs / by Jolanda G. Hengstman.
        p. cm.
    Includes bibliographical references.
    ISBN 0-7360-3375-0
    1. Movement education--United States. 2. Education, Preschool--United States 3.
English language--Alphabet--Study and teaching (Preschool)--Activity programs--United
States. I. Title.

    GV452 .H48 2001
    372.86'8--dc21

                                                                        2001016874

ISBN: 0-7360-3375-0

Lyrics of songs on pp. 27, 32-33, 42, 47, 53, 73, 91, 96, 104, 108-109 reprinted by permission from G. Stewart, 1987, *Animal walks* #9107 (Long Branch, NJ: KIMBO Educational).

Acquisitions Editor: Judy Patterson Wright, PhD; **Developmental Editor:** Jennifer Clark; **Assistant Editors:** Laurie Stokoe, Sandra Merz Bott, J. Gordon Wilson; **Copyeditor:** Barbara Walsh; **Proofreader:** Coree Schutter; **Permission Manager:** Dalene Reeder; **Graphic Designer:** Nancy Rasmus; **Graphic Artist:** Kathleen Boudreau-Fuoss; **Cover Designer:** Keith Blomberg; **Art Manager:** Craig Newsom; **Illustrator (interior and cover art):** Dawn Bates; **Printer:** Versa Press

Printed in the United States of America   10   9   8   7   6   5   4   3   2   1

Human Kinetics
Web site: www.humankinetics.com

United States: Human Kinetics, P.O. Box 5076, Champaign, IL 61825-5076
800-747-4457
e-mail: humank@hkusa.com

Canada: Human Kinetics, 475 Devonshire Road Unit 100, Windsor, ON N8Y 2L5
800-465-7301 (in Canada only)
e-mail: orders@hkcanada.com

Europe: Human Kinetics, Units C2/C3 Wira Business Park, West Park Ring Road, Leeds LS16 6EB, United Kingdom
+44 (0) 113 278 1708
e-mail: hk@hkeurope.com

Australia: Human Kinetics, 57A Price Avenue, Lower Mitcham, South Australia 5062
08 8277 1555
e-mail: liahka@senet.com.au

New Zealand: Human Kinetics, P.O. Box 105-231, Auckland Central
09-523-3462
e-mail: hkp@ihug.co.nz

contents

Preface   vii
Acknowledgments   ix

Part I   Framework for Language Stimulation in Movement Lessons

Characteristics of Young Learners   1
Planning   3
Implementing   4
Remaking, Recycling, and Reusing Materials   12
Practicing Safety   18

Part II   Movement Lessons

Understanding the Icons   20

Aa   A is for apple, ankle, arm, aerobics, and maybe even your name.
Try out the lesson routine, a good start is half the game.   21

Bb   B is for balls, balance, and balloons galore.
Create goals so everyone can score.   25

Cc   C is for clowning around and learning to clap, crawl, catch, and
other movements that matter while learning your letters.   31

Dd   Dancing the day away, what an idea, and learning our ABCs along
the way. Going down, dribble, duck, and drop—it's hard to stop.   36

Ee   We see with our eyes and hear with our ears. Exercise stations
and Elephant Swing are lots of fun, and the egg relay lets us run.   41

Ff   Fast and faster we go, and far and farther we throw.   46

Gg   "I see, I see something green." It is also for girls, gym, go, gallop, and glide.   52

Hh   Let's do the Hokey-Pokey, and a whole lot more.   57

Ii   We can form the letter with our bodies, it is us.
And ice cream or ice-skating are a must.   62

Jj Jogging and jumping up and down keep us fit.
Jingle bells on your shoes are a great hit! 66

Kk You are invited to go outside to fly a kite. Or stay indoors for a kicking course. 72

Ll Let's learn left from right as we go.
Tapping the lummi sticks or doing the limbo. 76

Mm The letter M moves to the marching band music and tumbles on the mats. 81

Nn Can we be nosy and noisy, and check out the news? 86

Oo The invitation to the Olympics is yours.
Try moving on, out, off, and over the obstacle course. 90

Pp Playing with the parachute with our partners in PE.
Learning about percussion for our musicians-to-be. 95

Qq Who is queen for the day? That's the question. And when
we are really quiet we can answer using gestures. 99

Rr After the races are run, and we've rock 'n' rolled like the best,
we deserve to relax and to rest. 103

Ss How about throwing snowballs? Or take your chance to
dance with spiders and scarves. 107

Tt The T is toe-tapping, tail-tagging, target-throwing, tennis-ball-tossing fun. 112

Uu The letter U goes up and under, and up and under all over the U.S.A. 117

Vv Who would not like to see themselves on video while moving
wearing vests, and playing volleyball at their best? 120

Ww Which way does the wind blow?
North, south, east, or west? Winter wonderland is where you might go. 124

Xx Design pathways and crossroads, play a game of tic-tac-toe,
and accompany the movements on a xylophone. 128

Yy The letter Y is part of the sign for "I love you."
We measure and jump a yard and learn to yo-yo, too. 132

Zz What a way to end: with a zoo. We have a zebra, and the elephant is
back, too. We zigzag from side to side. From beginning to end with pride. 135

Part III   Resources

Resource A Activities in Other Support Areas   140

Resource B Music and Songs   142

Resource C Handouts for Students to Take Home   144

Resource D Suggested Readings and Resources   153

References   155

About the Author   157

preface

For young children, movement is at the center of their lives. Young children acquire knowledge by manipulating, exploring, and experimenting with real objects. They learn almost exclusively by doing and by moving.

When I first presented the program of language stimulation via sensorimotor experiences with the teacher as facilitator, many attendees asked if the program was available in written form. Their questions indicated a need for this practical book. This is a need for purposeful movement that influences—and in turn is influenced by—motor, cognitive, and affective domains. There is a need for a developmentally appropriate movement program designed specifically for the younger child. Likewise, there is a need for a program that provides children with choices, can be individualized, and is all inclusive, so that children can seek out the stimuli they need to nourish their developmental abilities. *Movement ABCs* is written for those attendees looking for answers to meet their program needs. Most of these people are physical educators or adapted physical educators needing practical information. This book is also a great resource for special educators, preschool, Head Start, and kindergarten teachers as well as child-care providers, recreation leaders, and others working in formal settings with young children. Many activities do not require specialized equipment. In fact, they use easy-to-make equipment. Almost all activities can be done in small and large groups. The flexibility of the activities and their applications make this a unique book that will serve many professionals.

This program was formed out of a desire for increased language stimulation at the school where I worked several years ago. A new curriculum was designed that was based on the alphabet. This was the beginning of a multidisciplinary approach that fostered contacts between a number of disciplines such as classroom staff, art teachers, music teachers, speech-language pathologists, media specialists, parents, and physical educators. Both students and adults are enjoying the benefits of this integrated approach. Together with Connor-Kuntz and Dummer (1996) and Peter Werner (1996) I believe that we can integrate themes, in this case the alphabet, without losing the motor development component or sacrificing active movement.

Movement ABCs contains three parts. The first part provides the framework, emphasizing the characteristics of younger children. This part also provides guidelines for planning, and how the students' characteristics and the planning result in implementation. The implementation reflects appropriate practices as spelled out in the position statement of the National Association for Sport and Physical Education (NASPE, 1994). A list of adapted, reused, and recycled equipment is also provided to better meet the needs of younger students and those with special needs.

Part II provides the actual activities—the movement lessons, letter by letter. Each letter is divided into sections, and each section is identified in the book by its own icon. There is a list of words that begin with the particular letter. Suggestions for music are followed by activities that incorporate the suggested words. The activities are divided into warm-up, opening, stations, play area, and closing. The appropriate approach for the early childhood years is to use activities that focus on basic motor skills and movement concepts. This approach is in line with NASPE's position statement (1994) and is followed in this book. Teaching tips appear at the end of each letter and include adaptations for different levels of ability.

To assist you in your planning, part III contains information for other support areas, an alphabetized list of music used, handouts the students can take home, suggested readings and resources, and references.

Use as much of this book's information and ideas as your students need. As you plan your year ahead, try to facilitate at least 30 minutes of purposeful movement a day. To be able to provide daily movement, appeal to the multidisciplinary team you are working with. Ideally, this book will inspire your own creativity. Adapt and adjust as you see fit, and most of all, enjoy each moment with your students. Listen to your students; they have great ideas on how to adapt and adjust. Seeing the children understand and make connections will only encourage you to continue on the path of integrated learning, with movement at the center of youngsters' lives.

acknowledgments

I wish to thank those who became, both intentionally and unintentionally, my mentors for life and about life—those who encouraged me, told me I can do it; those who put life in perspective, taught me I am always in the right place at the right time. Thank you for your words, gestures, smiles, and touch. Thank you to Willemina Broekmate, Mannes Hengstman, Jos Hengstman, Gert van Driel, Dr. Howie Boyd, Catherine Bolton, Dr. Rick Duvall, Bill Anderson, Randolph Wilkinson, and Douglas Welton. I also owe thanks to Nancy Howie and Raygina Peak for developing the Alphabet curriculum for kindergartners at Metro School in Charlotte, North Carolina, and to all the students I had the great pleasure to meet and who let me teach and play.

PART I

Framework for Language Stimulation in Movement Lessons

Part I is the most important part of this book in that it makes you think about the premises from which you teach. This part discusses the reasons for an integrated curriculum, how such a curriculum benefits young learners, and how you can get it started by following National Association for Sport and Physical Education (NASPE) appropriate practices guidelines. Implementation of the integrated curriculum is based both on students' characteristics and on these appropriate practices.

Part I is also practical. It discusses how to create an integrated environment that facilitates students' motor development as well as language development. You will learn how to set up an area, use visual cues, design a routine, and make your own equipment. This part concludes with a section on safety, particularly in the selection of equipment and space.

Characteristics of Young Learners

Children want to move, children love to move, children need to move. In 1994 NASPE published five premises based on research and experience that need to be understood in any discussion of movement programs for young children. You too may have learned the following principles:

1. Three- to five-year-olds are different from elementary school-aged children. The focus must be on teaching the children rather than teaching

activities. This implies being able to adapt where needed to meet each child's needs, and remembering that form is not going to be perfect.

2. Young children learn through interaction with their environment. They need to be active participants, not passive listeners or observers. Movement concepts (body and space awareness, cause and effect) become functional and meaningful when practiced in the actual, natural situations.

3. Teachers of young children are guides or facilitators. Teachers set up an environment to elicit movement responses and guide the students toward the goals. Children are allowed to make choices, be creative, and explore. Predominant teaching strategies involved are movement exploration, guided discovery, and creative problem solving.

4. Young children learn and develop in an integrated fashion. Physical, emotional, social, and cognitive development are interrelated. The curriculum includes skills and concepts to enhance development in all areas. For example, ask questions to encourage cognitive development, encourage taking turns to enhance affective development, and work on colors by using colored balloons in activities.

5. Planned movement experiences enhance play experiences. Offer a combination of regularly scheduled designed movement experiences (intentional and purposeful), and regularly scheduled indoor and outdoor play experiences (more random and exploratory).

In short:

 Provide lots of repetition to give children lots of practice.

 Arrange active participation time for ALL children.

 Individualize activities by adapting equipment, instruction, and rules to facilitate success for all students.

 Have enough equipment (see the end of this chapter for ideas).

 Have few rules.

 Stick to those rules.

 Be organized.

 Stick to your organization and order of events; be consistent.

 Be silly; smile.

 Make sure everyone is a winner.

 Verbalize in short, clear terms to aid language development; use key terms and concepts.

 Know the purpose (goal) of your lesson.

Help students understand that having fun and trying are more important than doing something perfectly.

Young children's need to move supports their total development. Movement in an integrated setting where concepts become functional and language and cognitive development are stimulated provides the best learning environment for younger children. This conclusion that an integrated setting requires daily structured movement lessons for young children is shared by others. Steve Sanders (1996) agrees with the Southern Regional Education Board that younger children are not just smaller versions of older children. Younger children acquire knowledge in significantly different ways than older children do. They need to manipulate, explore, and experiment with real objects. In Connor-Kuntz and Dummer (1996), a study of four- to six-year-olds shows how language skills can blossom in an integrated setting, in this case a physical education class. They found that language skills can easily be implemented into physical education classes without sacrificing the physical skill development or taking up extra time. The following text provides instruction on how to create an integrated setting, include language development in the movement lessons, and become a team member of a multidisciplinary team.

Planning

Because facilitating language stimulation via sensorimotor experiences does not greatly affect your movement lessons but merely enhances them, you can implement the activities from this book on your own. This might be necessary if your administrator or colleagues do not give you the support you need. I do hope, however, that the experiences you and your students have help you find allies for this multidisciplinary approach to the curriculum.

When advocating for your vision of cooperation, share the information presented in the previous section, "Characteristics of Young Learners." You can also argue that having everyone work together will facilitate

 a wider knowledge base,

 mutual support,

 securing the best possible education for the students,

 problem solving,

 repetition and reinforcement of lessons taught in all areas, and

 starting this process at an early age to truly benefit the students.

Team Up With Colleagues

After the necessary discussions with teachers from other disciplines and your administrators, let's assume you have found support for your idea to follow a team-teaching approach for your young students. The alphabet is the theme, and you will present students with such concepts as direction, speed, distance, shape, color, and so on in a natural, functional environment.

At your first team meeting, set up a week-by-week calendar for the year, so that all disciplines involved will focus on the same letter and theme at the same time. This facilitates reinforcement and repetition across all areas. Some letters, such as "B," can take two or three weeks. You can also decide to change to a theme appropriate for, say, the week before winter break or the last weeks of the school year.

During the rest of the school year, meet regularly to share ideas on how to present certain letters, words, and concepts. Look to your classroom, art, and music teachers as great resources for ideas. Also use these meetings to evaluate. Written evaluations become guidelines for next year, help problem solve, and help create extra support for students who need it. This is also a great time to suggest what students can do during recess and free time and after school.

Share With Parents

Parents love to, and have a right to, know what their children are doing. Send an informative pamphlet home at the beginning of the year explaining the program. Have everyone involved write a short paragraph introducing themselves. During the year, keep the parents informed through weekly or monthly updates. These updates invite the parents to emphasize the same letters, words, and concepts at home that are being taught at school. Students' family members can also be great helpers when it comes to homemade equipment and discarded materials.

For an example of a letter to send to parents at the beginning of the school year and an example of a monthly update format, see Resource C. You will also find handouts with activity ideas in Resource C. Send these handouts home with students at specific times during the year. The handouts discuss and picture activities related to the air that we breathe, an exercise calendar, jump-rope skills, rhythm, rhymes, and measuring. When you follow the alphabet, the handouts will be spread out throughout the year.

Implementing

According to the dictionary, implementing means following up on a contract, a plan, or a promise. It is popularly known as "walking the talk" or "putting words into action." In this field it means "putting theory into practice." Implementation is based on students' characteristics and appropriate practices.

According to NASPE (1994), appropriate and inappropriate practices are defined through the following questions. The answers reflect the intentions of the program described in this book.

1. Is the curriculum based on children's interests and backgrounds?

   Yes, movement activities reflect age-appropriate choices for and by the children. A variety of experiences are created to teach the same motor skill in different situations. Repetition of basic motor skills happens throughout the year.

2. Are children allowed to make choices, discover, and create?

   Yes, the play area is created for this purpose. A large number of activities invite the children to be creative.

3. Are cognitive development and functional understanding of movement concepts addressed?

   Yes, activities allow for guided discovery by asking students questions. Many concepts are discussed, practiced, and explored throughout the curriculum.

4. Are social skills addressed?

   Yes, students are invited to be partners, to take turns, to share equipment where needed, and to clean up for the next person. Cooperation is stressed (parachute games, newcombe) instead of competition.

5. Is integration with other curricular areas present?

   Yes, specifically with language arts; hence this curriculum. Integration with math (counting, measuring, shapes), geography (learning about other countries), and science (flying kites, lungs, heart) are present.

6. Is the fitness component integrated as a fun part of moving, or is it a goal in itself?

   Throughout the warm-up, opening, and closing activities, fitness components are present. These are mostly indirect, and the focus of the activities is on movement skills.

7. Is ongoing, individualized assessment taking place?

   Continuous adjustments of the activities are possible to meet each student's needs. The curriculum has room for extra stations, or activities in the play area to address specific needs, and mentions equipment adjustments and choices. The children receive many opportunities to express themselves freely through word and movement.

8. Is active participation for every child maximized?

   Yes, the setup minimizes waiting time and ensures that equipment is plentiful. Equipment is supplemented by many homemade, nontraditional, recycled pieces.

9. Does the curriculum offer a variety of dance and rhythm experiences?

   Yes, the different types of music include rock 'n' roll, marching band, and limbo as well as student-generated music that uses songs, rhythm sticks, and percussion instruments.

10. Does educational gymnastics address broad skill areas?

    Yes, it continually addresses the skill areas of balance, rolling, jumping, climbing, and landing. Perfection of form is not required. The children learn to observe safety rules while having fun.

11. Are the games flexible in design, based on children's needs?

    Yes, each student can participate at his or her individual level. The emphasis is on participation rather than competition.

12. Is the success rate high?

    Yes, the adaptations suggested throughout the text facilitate success for all.

13. Are class size, frequency of movement instruction, and available facilities safe and appropriate?

    Ideally, yes. You will have to judge your particular situation and perhaps advocate for changes.

14. Are fine motor skills addressed?

    Yes, mostly in the play area during such activities as making newspapers, coloring eggs, and so on. Posters and blank paper with crayons are frequently part of the play area.

15.   Is information about the movement program shared with parents?
   Yes; see the parent handouts in Resource C.

We have come up with a workable situation based on these questions that allows children to participate fully at their highest level. Use the following ideas to build a framework for your particular situation.

Setting Up the Area

First and foremost, be ready and organized. It takes a few extra minutes to have all the stations, posters, and clues in place in the morning, but for the rest of the

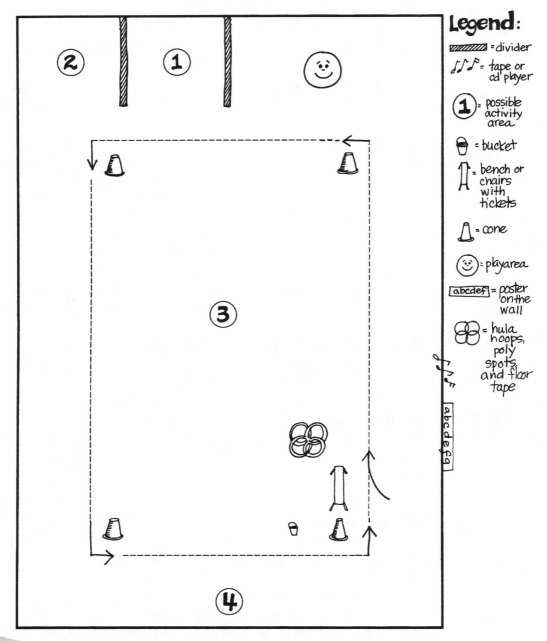

Figure 1   Layout of the equipment on the gym floor.

day you will be thankful (see figure 1, page 6). You have only one pair of hands, so try to get another adult to help you assist the students. The objectives are to make the area child-friendly and to facilitate easy, understandable transitions. The way you organize your equipment can make it easier to achieve these objectives.

For walking, jogging, running, or crawling laps, use cones to indicate directions as well as colored arrows taped to the cone or on the floor. Arrows on the floor need to be placed inside the lap so that students will not step on them. Pre-made laminated arrows work best and can be reused. To attach an arrow to a cone, extend the tape to the top of the cone, or make a small slit in the top of the cone and slide the arrow into it (see figure 2). If you do not have cones and pre-made arrows, you can use floor tape and lay down tape in the shape of an arrow on the floor. Another alternative to direct students is the use of yarn. Students follow the yarn.

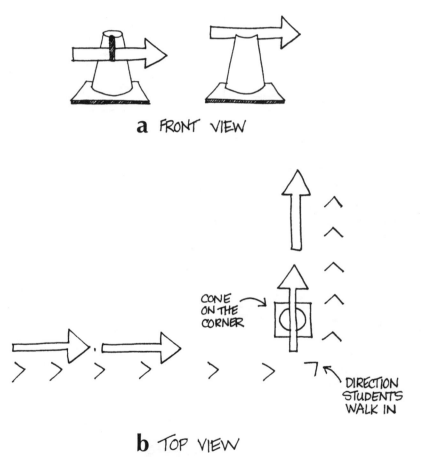

a FRONT VIEW

b TOP VIEW

Figure 2   The use of arrows for direction.
(a) Front view. Tape the arrow to the top of the cone or make a slit in the top of the cone.
(b) Top view. Arrows are placed inside the walking path of the students.

Once the children learn to follow the arrows, tape, or yarn and look for the cones, you can change the pattern. This may be necessary if you need more space for activities, or if the change in pattern is an activity in itself, challenging the students to pay attention. The colored arrows, tape, and yarn make the space look inviting (see figure 3, page 8).

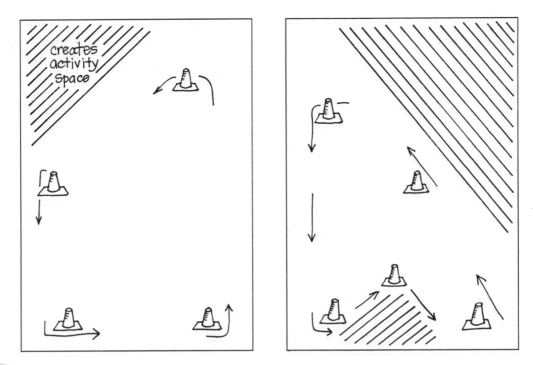

Figure 3   Use of cones to change warm-up path and create activity space.

To facilitate counting, number recognition, and independence, use a bench with small tickets placed on it. The tickets can be cutouts of the letter for the day, cutouts of multiple letters, or slips of colored paper. Also on the bench is a small poster with a number on it. This refers to the number of laps the students need to do and the number of tickets they can pick up. Sometimes students can be given the choice to use or not to use the tickets and be challenged to count the number of laps in their head. This is a way to differentiate between students who want or need the aid of visual cues and those who do not. There is a bucket on the other side of the bench for the students to put the tickets in, one at a time, at the end of each lap (see figure 4).

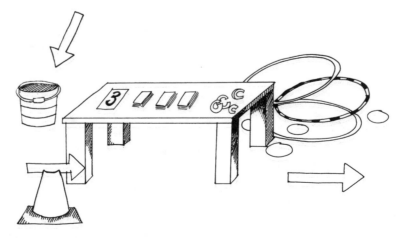

Figure 4   First thing the students see. Notice the arrows, the bucket, the bench with tickets and a number, and the hula hoops and poly spots waiting inside the warm-up path.

When there is no number, or the number 0 is on the bench, the children know to line up and not walk the laps.

Place room dividers between the play area and the activity area as well as between the two activity areas. Room dividers function as physical barriers, as visual barriers, and to keep equipment in or out. Balls, balloons, and things to juggle tend to move throughout your whole space. With dividers, the children know where to go and where to stay. You can decorate the room dividers with posters or with blank sheets of paper on which children can write or draw with crayons. Place a timer in the play area and perhaps in the activity areas as well. The play area is home to multiple activities and needs more space than the single-activity areas. You can have as many as 10 students at a time in the play area. Try to keep the balls out of the play area unless they are suspended.

Activities dealing with throwing at targets face the wall. This prevents the balls from rolling over the entire area. Have boxes and baskets available to put balls back into, or use a hula hoop to contain balls (see figure 5).

Get the tape player or CD player ready with a green dot on the start button and a red dot on the stop button. Use tapes that are 10 minutes in length (5 minutes on each side), and copy the music you need onto that tape. The short duration makes starting, rewinding, and restarting much easier.

Figure 5 Retaining balls.

Behind the bench are poly spots, hula hoops, and a roll of tape for students who want to mark their spot for the opening activity. These are also useful for students who need a visual reminder of where their personal space is.

Use posters to make your area child-friendly. You can use numbers or colors to identify stations, for example, "All students wearing a white shirt go to activity 2."

Use Visual Cues

Many young children cannot read yet but show interest in numbers, letters, colors, shapes, and words. Some can recognize letters, numbers, or whole words. This is also true for children who are developmentally delayed or have been diagnosed with autism. Students with autism need alternative ways of communication and need consistency. Visual cues often work well for them. The posters, signs, tickets, and colors used in the setup of the gym help all students understand and learn what is going to happen and what is expected of them. The use of signs and pictures also facilitates independence; your students can now read directions!

The tickets used to count laps help students stay on task. The task at hand is made very clear. For example, John has three tickets in his hand, and he learns to finish all tickets first before he can stop. The tickets also allow you to individualize. Challenge a fast student by telling her to do five laps (by handing her five tickets). Challenge a student who uses a walker to do two laps. When the sign says 0, no laps will be done.

The first student finishing the laps can turn on the music by pushing the green button (independently). After the children finish their laps, each finds a personal space and starts following the directions on the tape. Poly spots and hula hoops are great to mark personal space and can be ready for the students. Depending on the activity and student's ability level (one or two) chairs might be needed. For example, the sittercise exercises (letter S) are done from a sitting position. Not all students will be able to sit on the floor. Some need to sit in a chair.

The following are other visual cues used throughout the year:

 A timer helps a student to stay on task because it shows the student how long he/she has to do an activity. Little by little the time can be increased.

 A leaf on each student's left foot (see letter L)

 A red ribbon on each student's right foot (see letter R)

 Footprints for directions or to mark foot opposition for throwing

 Handprints for hand placement when rolling

 Lines marked on the wall to direct throwing or to mark the outlines of a goal

 A tree drawn on the wall (covered with Velcro) for reaching and bending to hang things

 A yardstick on the wall to measure jumping

 Measurements on the carpet to measure jumping

 High nets or lines to invite overhand throwing; low lines or going under nets to invite underhand throwing

 Posters to identify the stations by number or color

 Arrow, tape, yarn to indicate directions

 Posters and drawings of activities

 A choice board on the wall with pictures attached to it with Velcro. The pictures represent feelings and questions (see figure 6a).

 Aprons with Velcro on which the teacher can stick signs and pictures (see figure 6b).

 The teacher's posture, expressions, body language, and positioning

Design a Routine

As with the setup of the area and the use of visual cues, a routine helps you build the framework for your unique situation. Because no energy is lost on logistics such as starting, transitions, rules, and ending, this framework allows you to focus on the actual teaching and guiding of your students.

When students enter the gym, they know where to look for a cue (or clue) and can start the warm-up. The transition from warm-up to opening happens independently. A student turns the music on and finds individual space to exercise.

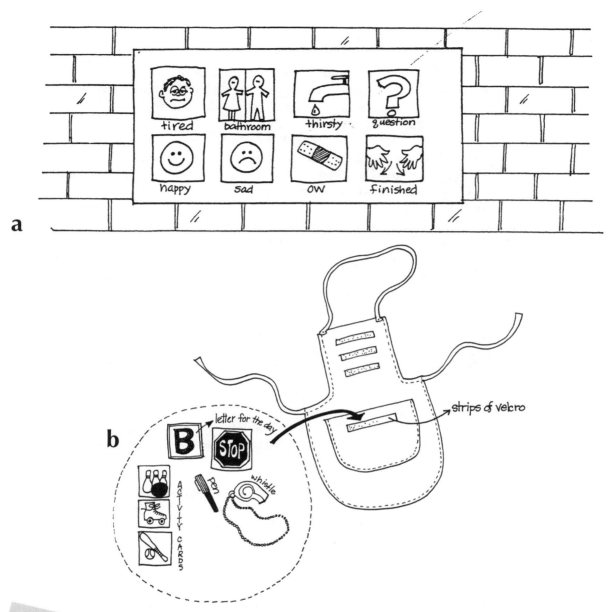

Figure 6 Visual cues.
(a) Picture board.
(b) Teacher's apron with Velcro strips. All the objects are kept in the apron pocket until needed.

When the opening is a circle activity, be ready with your hands out to the side to hold hands as the children file in to make the circle. Once all the children have finished the warm-up and have moved to the opening activity, change the music, add an exercise, or provide other variety within the framework of the opening.

After the opening, discuss the letter, color, special theme, or the like. Then divide the class into groups and send them to the stations where they practice, explore, make choices, and are creative.

Give a signal to indicate that it is time to switch stations. You can blow a whistle or stop the music, or a timer can go off. At the signal, students stop, clean up, and sit down. Use basic safety rules when switching stations. The phrases "Use your walking feet" and "Wait for instructions" are sometimes all you need to say.

The play area is a special station. When a group of students is assigned to this station, they are free to choose what to do. Most students discover many interesting ways to move, strike, kick, or balance on their own. Sometimes suggestions need to be made, and safety rules need to be clear and reinforced. The play area does not always have to rotate at the same time as the other stations; decide what works best for you.

Use a clear final signal to indicate the end of station time. The students stop, clean up, and come over to where the teacher is. It is best to get started with the closing activity as soon as possible, even if not all children have come over to the activity area yet. Getting started works as an incentive for those students to finish cleaning up their stations and join in with the closing activity. Use the last minute to repeat the letter for the day and verbalize the movements and activities learned.

Students who refuse to engage in the activities presented are either sick, do not understand the activity, or are not having fun. Not having fun is usually a result of the activity being "boring" (meaning too simple) or "stupid" (meaning too hard). Always remember that having fun is the top priority. If the students are not having fun, they are not going to learn.

Remaking, Recycling, and Reusing Materials

This list suggests some unconventional (i.e., not from a catalogue), cheap equipment. The list is not, and never can be, complete. Ideally, it will give you an idea of all the possibilities that exist and will challenge your imagination. To every problem there are creative solutions. Hint: ask, ask, ask. Ask parents or colleagues. Someone just might have that piece of equipment you are looking for in their basement. Don't forget the world's greatest invention: Velcro. When making posters, targets, and the like, laminate them so that you can use them again next year. Try to plan in advance. Look at the next letters of the alphabet to see if you need to start collecting items needed for the lessons, for example, newspapers and old socks.

Aerobic steps

 Pieces of carpet, planks, or boards make great low steps.

Balance beam

 Lines on the floor, a piece of rope on the floor, or boards make easy low balance beams.

Batting

 Use a ball on an elastic or rope, with the other end looped around the batting tee for easy retrieval. Use a cone for a batting tee.

Beanbags

 Make beanbags yourself out of nylon or sailcloth. Use different colors and shapes. Fill them with beans and decorate them with nontoxic permanent markers.

Bowling/bocce

 Use PVC pipe to create lanes.

Bubble blowing

 Use plastic hotel room keys that have holes punched in them.

Dividers

 Make dividers from large, opened-up cardboard boxes; gym mats placed on their sides; old room dividers from classrooms; or dividers from second-hand office equipment stores. To move the dividers (or any piece of large equipment), put scooter boards underneath.

Game nets

 Make nets out of soda six-pack rings and twist-ties. Ask grocery stores for twist-ties.

Incline mat

 Cover a piece of plywood with carpet. Raise one end up to create the incline.

Info board (transportable)

 Lace together three pieces of Peg-Board. Attaching Velcro makes it easy to put up information. You can also use a large, opened-up cardboard box (see figure 7a-b, page 14).

Lummi sticks (rhythm sticks)

 Have the hardware store saw 3/4-inch-diameter wooden dowels into 12-inch lengths. Use nontoxic paint to decorate and color them. Sand the edges smooth.

Ramps

 Use pieces of PVC pipe with a wide diameter. Students in wheelchairs can put a ball in one end of the pipe and have it roll out the other end toward a target. Use pieces of gutter material to build a more elaborate system of ramps (see figure 8a-b, page 15).

Rackets

 Short-handled rackets work best. Use table tennis paddles to bat balloons. Shorten badminton and tennis racket handles. If you do not like to use balloons, you can use beanbags or foam balls. To make a very lightweight racket, pull panty hose over a shape made from a metal clothes hanger. Watch for sharp edges. This type of racket is great for students with low strength.

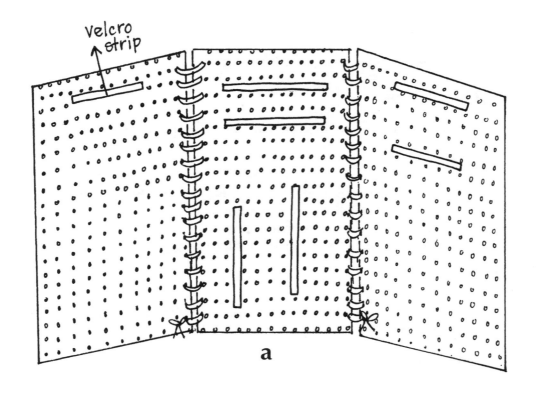

velcro
↑ strip

a

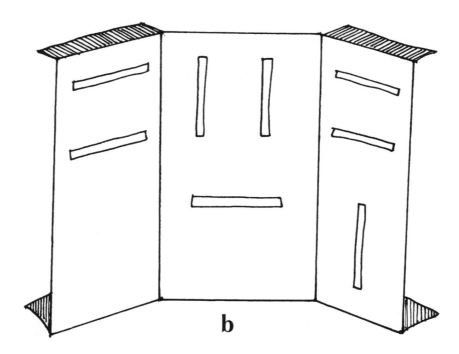

b

Figure 7 Portable information boards.
(a) Peg-Board laced together.
(b) Large cardboard box opened up.

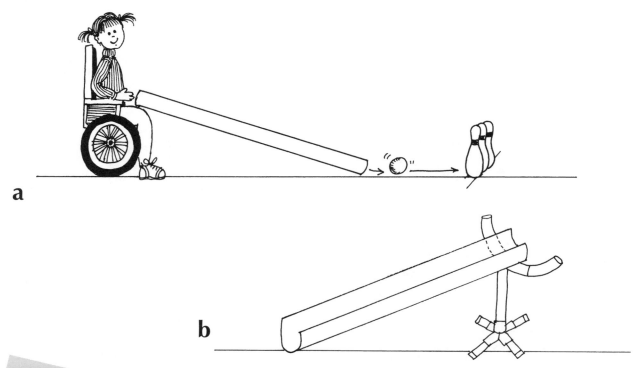

Figure 8 Gutters to enable all students to participate in rolling small balls.
(a) PVC pipe held on the student's lap so small balls can be rolled at the target.
(b) Open gutter to put balls in.

Ring toss

 Use bottles or blocks as pins, and use deck tennis rings or hula hoops as rings.

Rocking boards

 Make a rocking board by placing a sturdy board with smooth edges over a block. For a greater challenge, use a sturdy piece of pipe that can roll underneath the board (see figure R1 on page 105).

Roller-skating

 Roll out a piece of carpet to skate on to help students battle initial fear and balance problems. Replacing straps with strips of Velcro makes putting skates on easier and taking skates off faster, and students can do this independently. Put two strips of adhesive-backed Velcro back to back (sticky side on sticky side) and use one loop side and one hook side to make the new strap.

Jump ropes

 Buy a large spool of coiled rope. This investment will serve you well. You can cut the rope to any length you need. Tape the ends using masking tape to prevent them from unraveling. You can also use clothesline rope.

Rope bridge

 Drill holes in a plank and use rope to hang it between the parallel bars. Tie the rope with figure-8 knots; these are easier to undo than most other knots. Place footprints on the bridge to facilitate one-way traffic (see figure F1 on page 49).

Scooter boards

 Make a scooter board from a piece of wood with rounded corners and four casters or swivel wheels. Ask a hardware store to saw the wood, drill holes, and so on.

Snowballs and snowmen

 Use crumpled-up newspapers. Half a sheet in a sandwich bag makes a great snowball; lots of these in white trash bags can become a snowman.

Soccer

 Take an old ball net, cut out a piece large enough to fit around one soccer ball, and make a small, tight-fitting net. Attach a piece of elastic at least four feet long to the top and make a loop at the end of the elastic that fits around an ankle (see figure D2 on page 40).

Suspended balls

 Tie a sturdy nonelastic rope between two standards. Hang different objects from this rope as needed for ball or striking activities. Note the declining

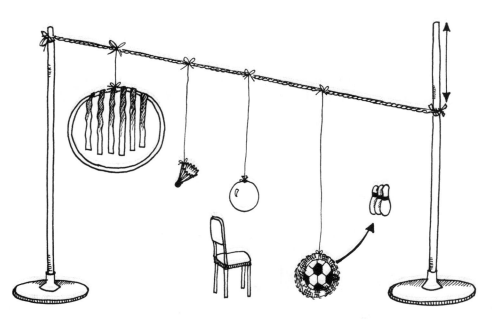

Figure 9   Suspending equipment. From left to right: hula hoop with streamers, a shuttle, a balloon and a chair for support, soccer ball in a net to be kicked at the bowling pins.

height of the horizontal rope (see figure 9, page 16). The vertical rope can be made from elastic or clothesline. We prefer a nonelastic rope because elastic bounces too much, making the path of the ball unpredictable. You can use any type of ball in this setting. A variety of balls facilitate participation for all students at all levels regardless of the unit you are teaching. For striking skills use tennis balls, Wiffle balls, or balloons at different heights. (When a balloon pops, make sure you pick up the pieces.) A small home-made net, made from an old ball net, is useful for hanging a soccer ball or basketball. Placing a goal or target behind the soccer ball can provide an incentive to kick in a particular direction.

Table tennis

 Use any table; do not worry about a net, and put two-by-fours (boards) up on the sides of the table to prevent the ball from rolling off. Nonambulatory students can play from their wheelchairs or can sit in regular chairs. A variety of paddles and balls are available, including table tennis paddles and balls. A Wiffle ball rolls more slowly than a table tennis ball, which usually enables students to be more successful. If needed, students can push the ball with their hands (see figure T1 on page 115).

Taps

 Tie bottle caps under students' shoes. Place the ragged edge against the sole of the shoe, not toward the gym floor.

Targets

 Set empty cans, bowling pins, and the like on a table.

 Turn a table on its side so that the balls disappear behind the table (see figure B1 on page 28).

 Use baskets, buckets, and boxes.

 Set up goals.

 Hang hula hoops and decorate them based on the letter or the season by hanging aluminum strips, paper leaves, colored balloons, or snowflakes in them.

 Hang targets from the basketball goal, in a doorway, or from a rope between two poles.

 Hang posters, pictures, or drawings, possibly with holes cut out.

 Draw targets, such as a tic-tac-toe grid, on pieces of carpet.

 Mark the spot from which the students throw with a movable marker such as a carpet square. Have the children throw toward the wall to prevent the balls from rolling away.

Throwing

 To facilitate repetition, tie a piece of elastic to a ball (Wiffle balls work great, or you can crochet a small net). With the other end of the elastic form a loop around the thrower's wrist.

Tunnels

 Use barrels, large cardboard boxes, or sheets draped over tables and chairs.

Practicing Safety

When making your own equipment, please make sure that it is sturdy and well constructed. Make sure there are no protruding nails, splinters, paint chips, or unstable pieces. A special warning applies to the use of balloons. If a balloon pops, please pick up the pieces as soon as you can because they are a choking hazard. Instead of balloons, consider using beach balls, foam balls, or cloth balls filled with packing materials such as foam packing peanuts. Racket activities also work with beanbags.

Safety is also a concern when you are setting up the area. Leave enough space between stations to prevent collisions. Use devices such as a table set on its side or dividers to contain balls. This prevents tripping and keeps the balls from rolling all over the floor.

Safety instruction needs to be a part of your routine. Repeat the applicable rules for that day, and demonstrate the appropriate use of equipment. Students move from station to station in a controlled manner (which means they must walk) after the equipment is put up and on the teacher's signal. Have a signal that tells the students to stop immediately, freezing in place.

You can find additional activity-specific information under "Teaching Tips" at the end of each letter in part II.

PART II

Movement Lessons

Part II puts theory into practice and is loaded with activity ideas. All activities are based on the appropriate practice guidelines as well as the characteristics of young learners as discussed in part I. Each chapter presents one letter of the alphabet, and the discussion is broken down into words, music, warm-up, opening, stations, play area, closing, and teaching tips as indicated by the icons. At the beginning of each letter chapter is a drawing of that letter. Copy the art and hand it out to the students as coloring sheets, or enlarge it, laminate it, and use it as a poster.

Under each letter you will find at least one activity that invites the students to distinguish between the uppercase and lowercase forms. The teaching tips at the end of each letter discuss safety, organization, and adaptations for students with disabilities or other limiting conditions.

Your particular situation, which encompasses the number and age of your students, the space and equipment available, curriculum requirements, and so on, will define which activities are appropriate for your use. Feel free to adjust, adapt, add, or alter the ideas given in this book. I hope they help spark your creativity. Be selective in choosing activities. Do not try to do them all, but select the ones that will guarantee success for all students.

Understanding the Icons

All activities for each letter are organized in subsections. Throughout the book, the following icons make it easier for you to find the subsections.

 **Words**

The words section provides a list of words that begin with the letter being studied. Many of these words will be repeated and emphasized in later sections such as in music and activities. This is a sample list; words can be added or deleted as appropriate.

 **Music**

The music section provides a list of songs that relate to the letter being studied. This list will be the recommended music for use in the other sections. Also, for added benefit, Resource A provides an extended list of music and songs that can be used as well. In addition, Resource B provides information on where the specific songs or music can be found.

 **Warm-Up**

The warm-up section will provide you with suggested warm-up activities that are tied to the letter being studied. These activities are designed to get the class ready to participate in more vigorous movement, while tying the warm-up to the letter being studied.

 **Opening**

The opening section is designed as the focal point for vigorous movement. The section provides detailed activities tied to the letter being studied on what to do during the beginning of the class to get the children started.

 **Stations**

The stations section provides a list of suggested activities to do at stations. The titles and descriptions of the activities are included for easy explanation to the class. Each activity relates directly to the letter being studied.

 **Play Area**

The play area is an area in which the students have various activities to choose from and participate in. Each chapter provides suggestions on what to include in the play area. The activities typically focus on tasks that enhance the learning of the letter being studied.

 **Closing**

The closing section provides a suggested activity to wind down the class. It will be the last activity before the class ends.

 **Teaching Tips**

The teaching tips section provides a list of tips on how to make the tasks or activities in the other sections easier and more refined to the letter being studied. It also suggests little things that can enhance the learning experience.

The Letter A

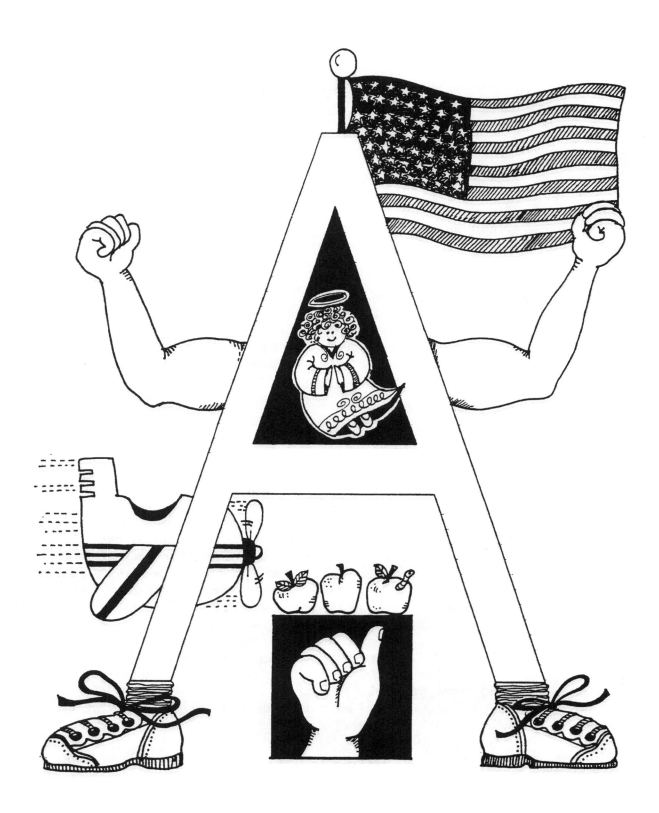

Words

Body parts: Ankle, arm

Nouns: Aerobics, air, airplane, America, angel, animal, applause, apple, activity, assistance, area, anything

Verbs: Ask, add

Directions: Above, across, after, ahead, around, at

Others: All, an, again, also, as, and, a, any, students' names that begin with A

Music

"Aerobics USA" by KIMBO Educational #8065

"Animal Walks" by KIMBO Educational #9107

"Electric Slide" from the CD "Christy Lane's Complete Party Dance Music"

"Rock'n'Roll Fitness Fun" by KIMBO Educational #9115

Warm-Up

Children walk or jog laps *around* the cones. *A* student whose name begins with A can wear the letter pinned on his or her shirt. Students can count the number of laps using cutouts of the letter A, or they can count in their heads. For each lap walked or jogged, each child places one cutout in a bucket (see part I: "Implementing").

Opening

Have the place marked where you want your students to go *after* their laps, *and* have a tape ready in the tape player. Establish your routine now! Use a tape that includes spoken verbal instructions. Most tapes from KIMBO Educational have this feature. A student who has finished the laps can turn the tape player on by hitting the button with the green dot. This facilitates independence, and the student can start with *aerobics* by following the instructions on the tape.

Once everyone has finished their warm-ups, you can choose to switch to the music selected for the letter A. Upbeat popular dance music such *as* the electric slide is also motivating. Design your own routine using *arm* and *ankle* motions by *asking* your students questions: "What can we do with our arms?" We can move them up, down, to the side, in front, behind our back, one arm up, one arm down, other arm up, tap the floor, tap your head, give yourself a hug, fly, and so on. "What can we do with our ankles?" Lift one ankle up, lift the other ankle up, touch your ankle, hold your ankle, and so on.

Point out that the letter A is for *air*. Invite the students to breathe in deep and breathe out. *Add* arm movements: raise your arms while breathing in, and lower them while breathing out.

The tape "Animal Walks" can be used. Point out that the A is for *Animal* and select a number of individual songs. Most songs are repeated *at* the end of the tape when we meet *all* the animals *again* in the zoo. This tape can be used for a variety of letters in addition to the letter A. For example, the "Elephant Swing" can be repeated for the letter E.

The students sign and verbalize the letter. Recognize words and students' names that start with the letter A.

Stations

Balance, jump down, hang/swing, tug

- Walk *across* the balance beam and put a Velcro star on the *American* flag. Verbalize turn taking: "John goes *after* Margaret, Margaret is *ahead* of John." *Also* specify the positions of the stars using the directional words listed earlier.

- Walk across the balance beam with your arms out to the side, like *an airplane*.

- Jump down like an *airplane* or an *angel*. Students can jump down from the end of the balance beam, aerobics steps, a vaulting box, sturdy plastic crates, or a bench (put these against the wall for stability).

- Hang by your arms and swing on a rope, a chin-up bar, or the parallel bars. Ask students, "How strong are your arms?"

- **Square Tug-of-War** (see figure A1).

  The rope is tied in a big circle so that there are no ends. Four students or groups of students hold it to make it look like a square. At a short distance from each corner is a cone with an *apple* on top. The object of the game is to reach the apple closest to you by pulling hard on the rope. Ask, "How strong are your arms?"

- Add *any* stations that represent individual objectives students need to work on.

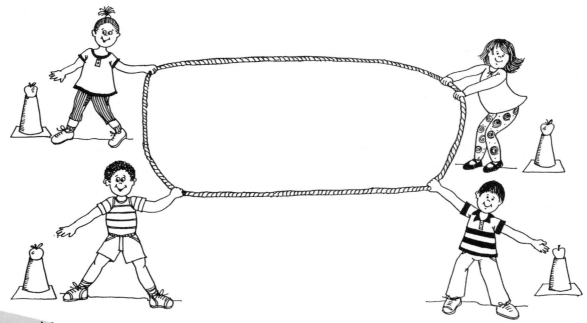

Figure A1 Square Tug-of-War. Notice the apples on the cones.

Play Area

Choose *activities* that students can do with little *assistance*. Students do need supervision, but let them choose which activity they want to do in the play *area* and how they want to do it. You might try having a variety of balance beams and boxes to jump down from. Have mats in place for the children to land on.

 Closing

Apple Race. "Help me pick all the apples and put them in the basket. Ready, set, go!" Put paper or plastic apples on the floor on one side of the gym. The students run to the apples, picking up one at a time and bringing it back to you. You can hold a nice basket for them to put the apples in. This is a great station to work on distinguishing between uppercase and lowercase letters. Half the apples have an uppercase A on them and the other half have a lowercase a. Children put the lowercase apples in one basket and the uppercase ones in another. There is *applause* and a pat on the back for all at the end.

 Teaching Tips

- In Resource C you will find a handout students can take home titled "A Is for the Air We Breathe..." This handout suggests activities children can do at home. It also includes a poem by the American Lung Association, along with the association's phone number.

- Keep the formations very simple. The letter A comes at the beginning of the school year. This means a basic warm-up of laps around the gym, aerobics in a circle, and the Apple Race from one end of the gym to the other and back.

- Young children need visual cues and directions. Use cones to mark the corners of the warm-up laps. Use carpets, chairs, or poly spots to indicate their personal space if needed.

- You can turn *anything* into a balance beam—a line on the floor, boards or planks of different sizes, or a long, narrow piece of carpet.

- Challenge and invite the students to turn around on the balance beam, to bend down and touch the beam, and so on.

- Elevate one end of the balance beam by putting an aerobics step or box under the plank or board.

- Place mats underneath the swing rope, parallel bar, chin-up bar, or other equipment that children hang or swing on.

- For square tug-of-war, establish a signal for everyone to stop and regroup when one apple is off a cone.

- Play tug-of-war with two or three students if needed—with three, the rope forms a triangle. Or play it with more than four students. The students hold onto the circular rope where they choose. Add cones with apples.

- Since red plastic apples are not available year-round, you can use paper cutouts of apples. Laminate them so that they can be reused.

The Letter B

 Words

Body parts: Back, body

Colors: Black, blue, brown

Nouns: Badminton, balance beam, balance board, balloon, balls (beach balls, bowling balls, basketballs), banana, basket, beanbag, bear, bicycle, block, box, bubbles, bucket, bunny, back

Verbs: Balance, bat, bike, blow, bounce, bowl

Directions: Backward, behind

Others: Big, bigger, biggest; students' names that begin with B

 Music

"Apples and Bananas" or "Bananaphone," both by Raffi, listed in the KIMBO catalogue

Song: "Old McDonald Had a Body" sung to the tune of "Old McDonald Had a Farm"

"Me and My Beanbag" by KIMBO Educational #9111

"Bunny Hop" from the tape "Animal Walks" by KIMBO Educational #9107

 Warm-Up

Throughout the lesson Teddy *Bear* can visit. This is left to the teacher's creativity. Some suggestions include:

- Teddy can be held during warm-up and where appropriate.
- Children repeat instructions to Teddy Bear.
- At the end of class, children explain what they learned to Teddy Bear.
- Teddy watches how everyone is doing a great job.

Stay within your established routine from last week. You can add *blue* (or *brown* or *black*) arrows on the floor, use blue (or brown or black) floor tape, or a blue (or brown or black) rope to follow. During part of the warm-up, have students walk *backward*. Use blue (or brown or black) cutouts of the letter B to count laps and for students to wear whose names start with the letter B. Mention the position of being *behind* someone.

 Opening

Have the place marked where you want your students to go after they finish their warm-up. Also have something ready for them to do, such as turning on the tape player and doing the beginning exercises as they did for the letter A. Once everyone is at the opening station, you can change and use the suggestions specifically for the letter B.

When using the Raffi songs, make up movements to go along with the words. For example, tap your hands on your knees, reach for apples and peel *bananas*, pick up and listen to the telephone. Remember, you're a physical educator; you can choreograph movements, and your students might have some great ideas, too!

When singing the song "Old McDonald Had a Body," change the words to, "And on that *body* he had two feet . . . with a kick-kick here and a kick-kick there . . ." Other suggestions: hand-shake, head-nod, shoulder-shrug, arms-reach, eye-wink, and *back*-pat.

The tape "Me and My Beanbag" and the song "Bunny Hop" come with movement instructions spoken on the tape. If you do not have a tape, make up a *beanbag* routine. Ask the students to *balance* the beanbag on a body part. Ask, "What other body part can we use? Can we move the body part with the beanbag on it?" and so on.

The "Bunny Hop" song has the following lyrics:

And now the *bunnies*

Here they come hopping along

Change feet

Two feet together, two feet apart [two times]

And off they go hopping along.

The song and music are flexible. The students can hop in a variety of ways and a variety of directions.

Students verbalize and sign the letter. They also recognize words and students' names that start with the letter B.

 **Stations**

Bat, balance, throw, kick, bike, roll, blow, bounce

- Suspend blue *balloons* (or foam *balls* or beach balls) at various heights from a rope. *Bat* the balloons (or balls) with either hand or a *badminton* racket. This can be done with a partner.

- Carry a blue ball across a balance *beam* to a blue *basket*. Ask, "Can you go backward?" See the letter A for balance beam ideas. You can also use upper- and lowercase blue, brown, and black cutouts of the letter. Place two baskets at the end of the balance beam—one for uppercase B and one for lowercase b.

- Balance *boards*. See rocking boards under the letter R for ideas. Depending on how the board is positioned on the support, the students can rock from front to back or from left to right.

- Throw balls or beanbags at a target. For targets, you can use empty cans, *boxes*, baskets, or *buckets* or suspended hula hoops with blue ribbons hung inside them. You can hang hula hoops from the *basketball* goal or from a rope between two standards. You can also turn a table on its side in front of a wall and throw the balls over the table. This retains the balls very nicely (see figure B1).

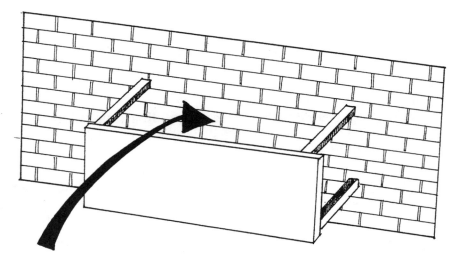

Figure B1   Table on its side as target.

- Kick a ball suspended from a rope (see figure B2).
- *Biking* on stationary *bicycles*, tricycles, hand cranks, table-top hand paddles, and so on.
- *Bowling.* Outline the lane using PVC pipe, which also functions as a bumper to keep the ball in the lane. Carpet squares mark the starting position, and blocks can be pins.
- *Blow bubbles* using plastic hotel keys with little holes punched in them.
- *Bounce* basketballs.
- Check to see if you need to do any activities related to individual student objectives.

Play Area

Expand the balance activities from the letter A with balance boards, and add the use of balls and colors. Ball activities where the balls are suspended, so they do not get in the way, are preferred.

Closing

It's Raining Balls. You sit on the floor holding a basket filled with a large number of tennis balls or other small balls. (Ask local tennis clubs to donate their so-called "dead" balls.) Try to empty the basket by throwing the balls everywhere while the students try to put the balls back in as fast as they can. Play according to their speed. Possible adaptations are using only half the gym, and throwing the balls shorter distances. If you need to use only half the gym, do so; do not throw the balls that far away and have two or more baskets available to return the balls.

Use the last seconds to repeat the letter and verbalize the activities the group has done. Also show the students the different balls used and ask questions related to *big*, *bigger*, and *biggest*.

Figure B2   Suspended objects on a rope of adjustable height.

 Teaching Tips

- Pick up the pieces of any popped balloons, or use foam balls, beanbags, or beach balls instead. The pieces present a choking hazard.
- Kids love colors. Use colored streamers, rope, tape, balloons, and paper any time you can to identify movement patterns (such as colored arrows taped on the floor), to assign groups ("All the children wearing blue stand next to the door"), or for targets.
- When inviting the students to walk backward, position yourself at the end of the lap to prevent them from walking into the wall or an obstacle.
- Young children are more successful with rackets that have short handles. They can use table tennis paddles to bat balloons, or you can shorten the handles on badminton rackets.
- Always practice the song and listen to the music before you use it in class.
- Have students practice counting skills while batting the suspended balloons and balls.
- By suspending balls, hula hoops, and the like from a rope between two standards, you can easily adjust the height. This will make the batting and kicking stations accessible to students in wheelchairs.
- At the kicking and batting station, students with balance problems can benefit from practicing while seated in a chair.
- A wide piece of PVC pipe can function as a ramp for students who need to sit at the bowling station. They can place smaller balls into the top of the pipe that roll out at the bottom toward the pins or blocks.
- Do you have any "Beary Good" stickers?

- Footprints or poly spots facilitate opposition when students throw or roll the ball.
- At the throwing station, have as many balls available as possible. I have buckets with at least 10 balls in each available. A student throws all the balls (until the bucket is empty), gathers them back up, and either throws again or puts the bucket down for the next person.
- Ask college or professional teams to donate minibasketballs to your program.

The Letter C

Words

Nouns: Can, carpet squares, cat, caterpillar, circle, clown, cocoon, cone, corner, crocodile, cutout

Verbs: Catch, clap, crawl, creep, curl

Directions: Center, close

Others: Students' names that begin with C

Music

"Clap Your Hands to a Groovy Beat" from the tape "Hand Jivin'" by Educational Activities Inc.

"Cat Stretch," "Crocodile Creep," and "Caterpillar-Cocoon-Butterfly," all from the tape "Animal Walks" by KIMBO Educational #9107

"Surfin' USA" (the directions on the tape ask for clapping) from the tape "Rock 'n' Roll Fitness Fun" by KIMBO Educational #9115

Warm-Up

When the students come in, give them a red *clown's* nose, after which they start the basic routine of jogging or walking the laps. Invite the students to perform different movements on each leg of the warm-up lap. For example, to get to the first *corner* (marked with a *cone*), *clap* hands; to get to the second cone, *crawl*; to get to the third, *creep*; and to get back to the beginning, *curl* up. Have *cutouts* of the letter C handy for students whose names begin with C or who need to use the cutouts to keep track of the number of laps completed.

Opening

You can use the established routine first or start with the suggested music, which has the instructions spoken on the tape. Form a *circle* and ask for one or more leaders to go to the *center*. This is a good time to introduce the letter, the sign language sign, and the directional concepts of center and *close*.

The song "Clap Your Hands" introduces different levels to clap (high, low) and positions (behind your back, to your side). "Surfin' USA" has exercises such as kick, clap, jump, and march.

The "Cat Stretch" song has the following lyrics:

Here comes the *cat*

Hands on the floor

Stretch one leg back

Now walk 2, 3 stretch [four times]

And again.

You can add other stretches to the movement pattern.

The "Crocodile Creep" song has the following lyrics:
Here comes the *crocodile*
Hands on the floor
Legs stretched back, ready and
Creep 2, 3, 4, 5, 6, 7, 8 [three times]
Sit up 2, 3, 4
Arms out 2, 3, 4
Open 2, 3, 4, 5, 6
Begin again.

Ask, "What other movements can a crocodile do?"

The "Caterpillar-Cocoon-Butterfly" song has the following lyrics:
First comes the *caterpillar*
Hands on the floor, legs straight
Walk with the hands and stop
Walk with the feet and stop
Now the *cocoon*
Curl up small
Wrap your arms around you and stay very still
Then out comes a beautiful butterfly and flies away.

Stations

Crawl, Creep, Catch, Throw

- Crawl or creep through a barrel, through a large cardboard box, through a tunnel, under a sheet pinned to two chairs, under a table, under a rope taped over two cones, or over or across a mat or incline. (Students can take upper- or lowercase cutouts of the letter C with them and place them in the appropriate basket.)
- *Catch* balls individually; add the challenge of clapping hands before catching the ball again.
- Throw the ball against the wall and catch it (see "Wall ball" under the letter W).
- Throw and catch the ball with a partner.
- Throw balls at *cans*.
- Throw balls through the holes in a large wooden cutout of a clown.
- Design an obstacle course that uses the movements of crawling and creeping on pathways of *carpet squares* (see figure C1). This is an opportunity for the students to distinguish between the upper- and lowercase letters. They can take along either an upper- or lowercase cutout and place the letter in the appropriate basket at the end of the obstacle course.
- Any other activities you need to work on based on students' individual needs.

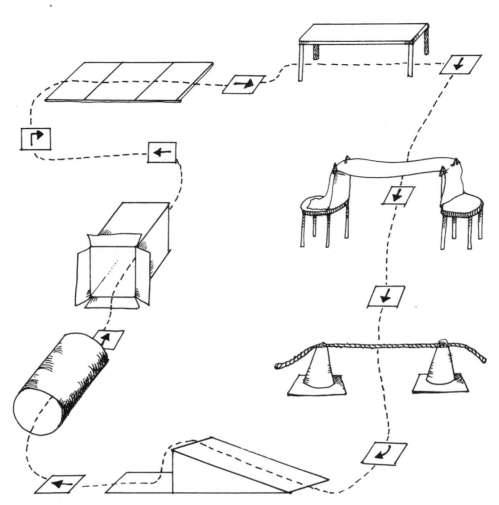

Figure C1   Crawling through and over objects in an obstacle course.

Play Area

Use the obstacle course (see figure C1) as well as the activities used for previous letters. An obstacle course set up in a circle works well in the play area. It is a repetitive activity. When the student finishes the course, he or she is back at the beginning and can follow the course again.

Closing

Students love the **Caterpillar Crawl**. They get on their hands and knees and make a long line, each holding onto the ankles of the student in front of him or her. They all need to work together to crawl forward. The more students in the line, the harder it gets!

Finish back in the circle to repeat the letter for this lesson.

Teaching Tips

- When asking the students to perform different movements during their warm-up laps, adjust the distance from cone to cone (corner to corner) to help them succeed. The lap will look not like a square but more like a trapezium.

- To maintain the shape of the circle during the opening of the lesson, have each student mark his or her own space using a carpet square, poly spot, or piece of tape.

- Put hula hoops down as boundaries and to mark individual working space where needed.

- When introducing catching with a partner, have overactive students sit down first to facilitate early success. After a number of successful catches, let them stand up and catch the ball.

- Increase success in catching for students with visual impairments by using brightly colored objects. Yellow and orange are good choices. Various equipment companies sell bell balls. A bell ball has an audible device, such as a jingle bell, inside. A student with a visual impairment can hear where the ball is.

- Start the Caterpillar Crawl with small groups of only two or three students.

The Letter D

 Words

Nouns: Dance, dog, duck
Verbs: Dance, dodge, dribble, drop, duck
Directions: Down
Others: Students' names that begin with D

 Music

Song: "Old McDonald Had a Farm"
Any type of dance music, including the suggestions made for previous letters
Specific music styles: Rock 'n' roll, Latin music, square dance music
Christy Lane's dance music collections available through Human Kinetics and listed in Resource D

 Warm-Up

Use cones to mark the corners of the warm-up laps. On their way to the first cone, students pretend they are *dribbling* a basketball; to the second cone, they move arms up and *down*; to the third, they dribble the basketball again; and to the last, they move arms up and down again.

You can also use the *dance* music that you will be using later in the lesson. When the music is playing, the students walk or jog their laps. When the music stops, they stop right where they are. When you turn the music back on, they can continue. Repeat this sequence.

Have cutouts of the letter D available for students whose names start with D or for those who need to count the laps to help them stay on task.

 Opening

Sing the song "Old McDonald Had a Farm." Old McDonald had a *dog* and a *duck* on his farm. Make the sounds these animals make as well as the movements. You can add other movements as well: form the shape of a house or farm with your hands in the air; point with a finger on "here," "there," and "everywhere."

Use the dance music. How about some great rock-n-roll music and moves? Or do you prefer the limbo set to Latin music? Maybe circling on some square dance music?

Rock-'n'-Roll Ideas

Twist your body.

Twist your body and support the movement with your arms.

Twist your body and move down.

Twist on one foot, then the other.

Twist on one foot and turn around.

Direct the level of the movements by showing an uppercase D or a lowercase d. The uppercase letter means stand/dance/twist up high (stand tall), and the lowercase one means dance/twist/move down low.

Limbo Ideas

Hold the rope or stick at a decreasing height.

Hang the rope between two standards or from the backs of two chairs at different heights.

Square-Dance Calls

"Say hello to your neighbor on the left and the right."

"Circle to the left." (While holding hands in a circle, everyone moves to the left.)

"Circle to the right." (While holding hands in a circle, everyone moves to the right.)

"Arms up with a hoot and a holler." (Everyone says "Yee-hah!")

"Into the middle and back." (Everyone moves to the center of the circle, then back out.)

"Marie, weave." (Marie, or any other student, moves in and out of the circle until she is back at her own place; see figure D1. More than one student can weave in and out at the same time.)

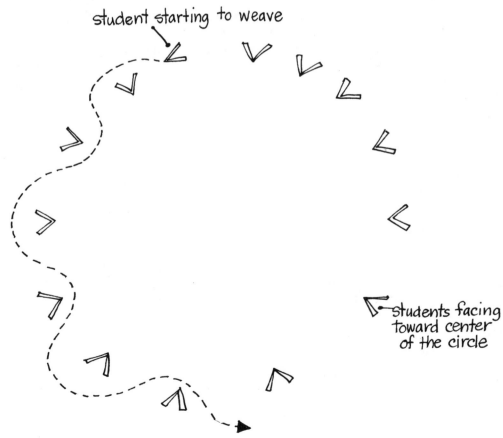

student starting to weave

students facing toward center of the circle

Figure D1 Weaving in and out of the circle.

Introduce the letter, the sign language sign, and recognize words and names that start with D.

Stations

Throw, dribble (basketball and soccer ball), dance, dodge/duck

- **Dog Bone Toss.** Toss dog bones (real or plastic) toward targets such as buckets, over a table on its side, through a hula hoop, and so on. Have a broom handy for cleaning up after class.
- Dribble a basketball. Challenge your students by counting how many times they can dribble in a row. Demonstrate the following choices: dribbling with both hands, dribbling with the left hand, dribbling with the right hand, and walking while dribbling.
- Dribble a soccer ball toward a goal, or follow a path such as around the cone and back.
- **Soccer Bowling.** Dribble the soccer ball toward a goal with bowling pins on the goal line. Designate a line from which the students are allowed to shoot on goal.
- Dance. See the suggestions under "Opening." The limbo dance is very suitable for small groups, or you can simply invite the students to dance freely.
- *Dodge* and *duck* in small groups such as two on two, one on two, or one on one. See "Teaching Tips."
- Any activities that need to be repeated from previous lessons or are necessary based on individual students' needs.

Play Area

Set up multiple limbo situations at different heights. Turn on the music and let the children have fun. They can practice the limbo or dance freely.

Closing

This game is called **Freeze**. Turn on upbeat dance music and invite the students to dance. The moment you stop the music, the students have to "freeze," or stop immediately. When you turn the music back on, they can resume dancing. After the dance, close with repeating the letter.

Teaching Tips

- Where possible, perform the circle dances in smaller groups with an adult in each circle.
- A basic movement to introduce dribbling a basketball is to hold the ball in front of the student and ask him or her to push the ball down.

- To keep balls from rolling all over the place when introducing dribbling a soccer ball, put the soccer ball in a net. Attach the net to the student's ankle with a piece of elastic that is at least four feet long. Know the student's preferred kicking foot and use that ankle. You can make these small nets out of pieces of a larger ball net (see figure D2).

Figure D2   Soccer ball in a net for dribbling.

- For dodging, use a small, clearly marked area. Cones, rope, or walls can mark the borders for the area. The tagger wears a pinney or ribbon. A dodger who gets tagged switches places with the tagger. The simplest setup is to have the dodgers run from a point behind one line to a point behind another line, with the tagger waiting in between. Players are safe behind the line.
- Check your local school supply store for stickers with dogs on them.

The Letter E

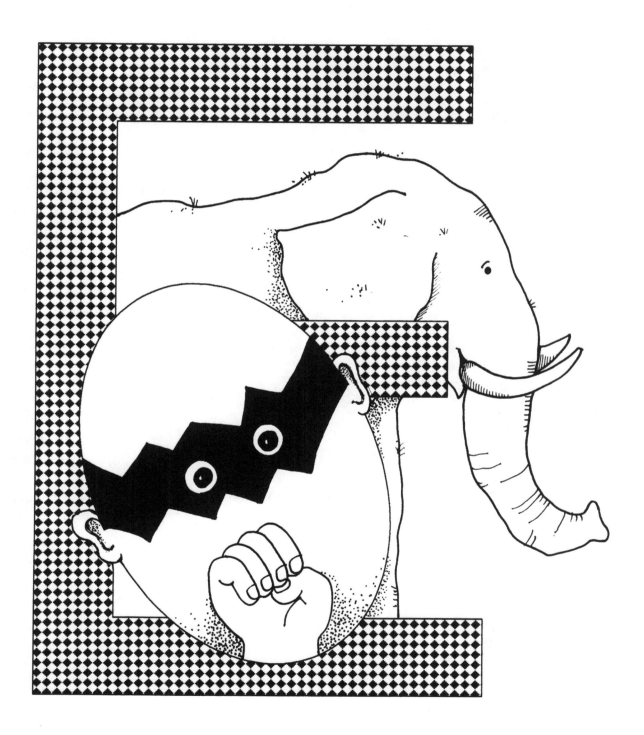

Words

Body parts: Ears, eyes

Nouns: Easter, egg, elephant, exercise

Verb: Exercise

Direction: End

Others: Each, empty, students' names that begin with E

Music

Song: "Head, Shoulders, Knees, and Toes." Emphasize the words "eyes" and "ears."

"Elephant Swing" from the tape "Animal Walks" by KIMBO Educational #9107

Song: "We're Jumping Up and Down," sung to the tune of "The Farmer in the Dell"

Exercise music: any upbeat popular music

Warm-Up

Turn the warm-up routine into an *egg* walk or egg run. Place a basket or bucket filled with plastic *Easter* eggs at the beginning of the warm-up lap. Try to have at least three eggs for each student. *Each* student takes one egg out of the bucket as he or she passes it and at the *end* of the lap puts it in the *empty* bucket. The whole class continues jogging or walking laps until all the eggs are gone.

Opening

Sing the song "Head, Shoulders, Knees, and Toes," emphasizing the part about *eyes* and *ears*.

> The "Elephant Swing" song has the movements spoken on the tape. The song has the following lyrics:
>
> Here comes the *elephant*
> Stand up, feet apart
> Bend over, hands together
> And walk
> Swing your trunk from side to side
> Reach up overhead
> Bend down through your legs. [Last two lines twice.]

Ask the students for additional elephant movements.

> Sing "Let's Jump Up and Down."
> The song has the following lyrics:
> Let's jump up and down.
> Let's jump up and down.

Exercise is what we do.

Let's jump up and down.

For additional verses, replace the line "Let's jump up and down" with the following:

Let's bend and touch our toes.

Let's kick our legs up high.

Let's run real fast in place.

Let's stretch up to the sky.

Play any kind of upbeat exercise music and make up an exercise routine. Ask students to come up with movements, but be prepared to introduce some movements yourself to get the activity started.

Examples of exercises: arms up/down, one arm up/down, march in place, circle your arms forward/backward, jump, kick, knees up, jumping jacks.

Introduce the letter, the sign language sign, and mention words that begin with the letter E.

Stations

Aerobic exercise, throw, balance

- Exercise station. You can use one of the general aerobic tapes with the workout spoken on the tape (see suggestions in resources B and D).

- **Egg Toss.** Use the plastic eggs from the warm-up. Tape them so that the two halves do not come apart. Toss the eggs onto something soft such as a mat, or into a basket with crumpled paper on the bottom.

- Throw at suspended targets made of paper or plastic eggs or decorated with eggs.

- Hide the eggs and invite students to find them. Or have one group of students hide them for another group.

- **Egg-on-Spoon Walk.** Starting with a basket filled with plastic eggs, each student puts one egg at a time on a spoon, walks it over to another basket, and places it inside. Direct the students over a balance beam or through an obstacle course using directional concepts. For example, they can go around cones, over a rope, under a table, across a mat, over an aerobic step, and so on. Have cutouts of both the uppercase and lowercase letters available, or mark the eggs with either upper- or lowercase E. The students need to place the letter in the correct basket.

- Do you need to repeat any stations from previous lessons?

Play Area

Put paper on the wall in the shape of an egg. Use a large sheet of paper or multiple sheets. Have crayons and pencils available for children to decorate the eggs. A second suggestion for the play area is an obstacle course with a circular layout.

Closing

You can do a variety of activities depending on the level of your students and your class size. Some of the station activities are suitable for the closing as well.

Hide all the plastic eggs and have the students try to find them.

Students balance an egg on a spoon and move around freely, thus working on spatial awareness. Suggest movements such as turning around, touching the floor, smiling, walking on your toes, and the like.

Egg Clean-Up. Put all the eggs on the floor on the far end of the gym. Show the students an empty basket or egg carton and ask them to help you refill it. They run to the far end of the gym and bring back one egg at a time until all the eggs are in the basket or carton.

All Ears. One student is It and sits in the middle of the gym on the floor, facing away from the other students. Tell this student, "Close your eyes and open your ears." The other students line up on one side of the gym. You point to a student who then tiptoes, as quietly as possible, to the middle of the gym and sits down behind It. You can point to as many or as few students as you wish. Then ask It how many students are sitting behind him or her (see figure E1).

Figure E1   The game All Ears. Selected students quietly sit down behind one student.

Teaching Tips

- In Resource C you will find a handout titled "E Is for Exercising." You can send this handout home with students. It is a 30-day calendar with an exercise for each day.

- If you cannot find enough plastic eggs, use laminated paper shapes. Students can make these in the classroom or during art and can decorate them. Table tennis balls can be pretend eggs.

- An economical time to buy plastic eggs is after the Easter holiday.

- To individualize the station where students carry eggs on spoons, you can use different-size spoons and different-size eggs, or have students carry the eggs by hand. The most important part is the physical activity of balancing or crawling through the obstacle course.

The Letter F

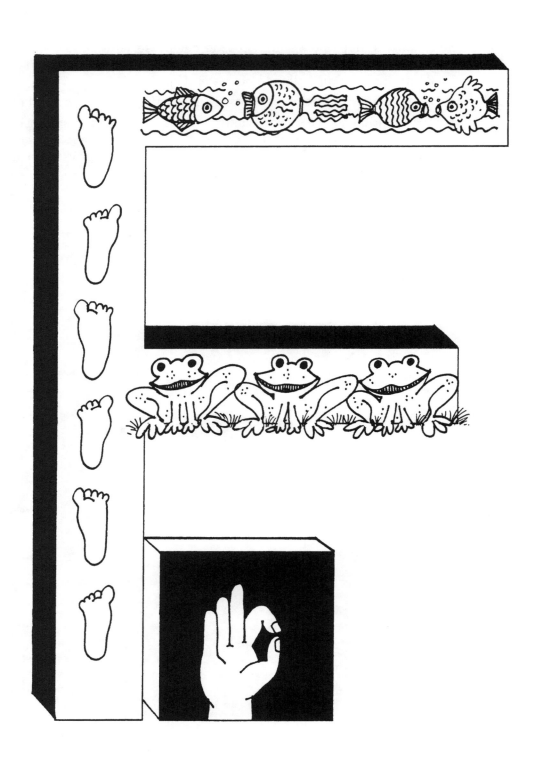

 Words

Body parts: Face, feet, fingers, foot
Nouns: First, fish, flexibility, floor, food, frog
Verbs: Fall, fish, follow, freeze, frown
Directions: Far, farther
Others: Fast, faster, students' names that begin with F

 Music

"Sittercise" by KIMBO Educational #2045
"Frog Frolic" from the tape "Animal Walks" by KIMBO #9107
Song: "This Is the Way," sung to the tune of "The Wheels on the Bus"
Song: "My Foot Can Touch My Nose," sung to the tune of "The Farmer in the Dell"
"Finger Play" from the tape "Hand Jivin'" by Educational Activities Inc.

 Warm-Up

Talk about *feet* and *fast*. Make pathways with *footprints* if you can.
Play **Follow the Leader** either as a whole class or in small groups.
Have cutouts of the letter F ready for students whose names begin with F or for students to keep track of the number of laps they have done.

 Opening

The "Sittercise" tape offers a variety of movements for both arms and legs (ask, "What can we do with our feet?"), done in a sitting position. Movement instructions are spoken on the tape.

"Frog Frolic" has movement instructions spoken on the tape. The song has the following lyrics:
Here's the *frog*
Hands on the ground, bend your knees
Now bounce, 2, 3, 4, bounce, 2, 3, 4
Hand, jump [eight times]
Place your hands, place your head
Knees on your elbows, balance. [Repeat from "Now bounce." When repeating the music, you can substitute other frog movements that the students suggest.]

When singing "This Is the Way," make up your own movements. The first verse is as follows:
This is the way we *frown* our *face*, frown our face, frown our face
This is the way we frown our face, early in the morning.

Repeat, replacing "frown our face" with *"fish* for *food,"* *"fall* to the *floor,"* "stamp our feet," and so on.

The song "My Foot Can Touch My Nose" has the following lyrics:

My *foot* can touch my nose

My foot can touch my nose

Just you wait and see me bend

My foot can touch my nose.

For other verses, replace "my nose" with "my head," "my elbow," "my toe," "my knee," "my foot," and so on.

The song "Finger Play" asks children to move individual *fingers* as well as the whole hand. It also talks about left and right. Students can come up with their own movements, too.

Guided discovery. Ask, "What can we do with our feet?" Have students give you suggestions. One student demonstrates and the other students *follow*.

Locomotor skills across the gym. Ask, "How can our feet get us from this side of the gym to the other?" We can walk, run, tiptoe, go backward, go sideways, gallop, hop, skip, leapfrog, and so on.

Together with the students, verbalize and sign the letter. Recognize words and names starting with F.

Stations

Jump, kick, balance, push, walk, cycle, skate, fish, throw

What Can We Do With Our Feet?

- Trampoline: We can jump with our feet. Use small jogging trampolines.
- Soccer: We can kick with our feet. See the suggestions for dribbling under D and kicking under K.
- Balance: We follow the footprints on the balance beam; we follow the footprints on the rope bridge (see figure F1).
- Push: We can push a scooter board with our feet.
- Walk: We can walk with shoe boxes on our feet; we can walk on cans (see figure F2).
- Cycle: We can cycle with our feet on a tricycle or bicycle.
- Skate: We can roller-skate with our feet; we can ice-skate with socks on our feet.

Other Stations

- **Go Fish.** Make fishing rods out of sticks or bamboo poles, with a small magnet at the end of the line. Use a large cardboard box, a children's inflatable swimming pool, or gym mats put on their sides as a fishing bowl. Make fish out of paper with metal washers. The magnet pulls the metal washer and the fish is caught. Some fish can have the uppercase F on them and some can the lowercase f. Students put the two in different buckets.
- Throw *far* and *farther*. For target ideas, see under the letter B.

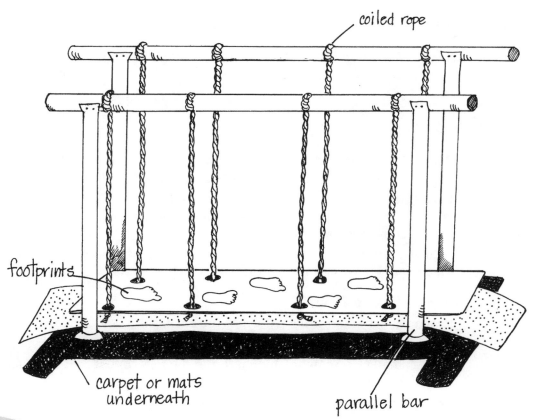

Figure F1 The rope bridge or swing bridge.

Figure F2 Walking with shoe boxes and on cans.

Play Area

Make a circle of activities done with the feet. Include balance, jumping, and kicking a suspended ball. Direct the flow of traffic by using footprints.

Closing

Repeat the locomotor skills mentioned in the opening section.

Repeat the game *Freeze*, mentioned under "Closing" for the letter D (see page 39).

Play **Follow the Leader**. Divide the students into small groups and assign a leader. Everyone in the group has to follow the leader. The leader has to make sure everyone can follow the pace.

Relaxing and stretching for *flexibility* is a great way to calm down at the end of the lesson. Here are some simple stretches:

In Standing Position

Reach up with your arms (stretches the back, sides, and arms).

Put your hands together behind your back (stretches the chest and shoulders).

Take a small step with one foot and pull the toes of that foot up. Then do the other foot (stretches the calves).

Lean your head to one side on your shoulder and switch to the other side (stretches the neck).

In Sitting Position

Put the soles of your feet together and push your knees out and down (stretches the inside of the legs).

Lie on your back and bring both knees up to your chest (stretches the lower back).

Lie on your back with one leg straight on the floor and the other straight up in the air. Switch legs (stretches the hamstrings).

Roll over on your stomach, bring one foot up to your buttocks, and hold your ankle. Switch legs (stretches the quadriceps).

Cat stretch—come up on all fours and arch your back (stretches the back). Alternate between arching up (say, "Tuck your chin") and arching down (say, "Look up").

Repeat verbalizing, signing, and discussing words that begin with F.

Teaching Tips

- Follow the Leader can be a warm-up, opening, station, or closing. It can be played in small groups where one student is the leader and the others follow, or even in pairs. The most important rule is that the leader cannot run away from the other students. The leader has to make sure that everyone follows, adjusting the pace.

- Be a leader yourself and demonstrate different locomotor movements and arm movements for your group to follow. This will give the student leaders ideas, and it allows them to be creative as well. Rotate the leader so that every student gets a turn.

- Make footprints from nonslip material used to line kitchen drawers and under area rugs. You can also draw or paint footprints on mats or pieces of carpet.

- When choosing multiple stations where students move between them, guide the students in a single direction to prevent collisions. For example, instruct them to go from one side of the gym to the other, turn around, and come back.

- At the stations, emphasize the word *first*, which starts with F: "Who goes first?"

- If students are waiting at the trampoline, set a maximum number of jumps.

- Use mats underneath the rope bridge, and have students cross it one at a time.

- Make the rope bridge by hanging a plank between parallel bars. Using coiled rope and figure-eight knots will allow you to undo the knots when needed. Ask a local hardware store to drill the holes in the plank (see figure F2).

- Short ropes held tight make walking on cans easier. I get cans from the school cafeteria. Be careful about the cans' potentially sharp edges!

- When stretching, count out loud clearly, at least to 10.

The Letter G

 **Words**

Colors: Gray, green, gold

Nouns: Garbage, garden, ghost, giraffe, girl, goal, gym(nastics)

Verbs: Gallop, glide, go

Others: Good, great, students' names that begin with G.

 **Music**

Halloween music is usually appropriate by the time we get to the letter G. If your school's social structure allows it, include songs about *ghosts* (G is for ghost).

"Giraffe Skip" from "Animal Walks" by KIMBO #9107

 Warm-Up

Mark the warm-up path with *green* (or *gray* or *gold*) arrows, green (or gray or gold) yarn, or green (or gray or gold) tape, and use green (or gray or gold) cards to count the laps.

While students do their warm-up you can talk about doing a *good* or *great* job. Designate part of the warm-up for *galloping*. Play Halloween music, if it is allowed, in the background, and turn the lights low.

 Opening

If you use Halloween music, you can dance with sheets, cloths, or pillowcases. You can direct the "Friendly Ghost Dance" or let the students be creative. If students are worried about putting sheets over their heads, they can drape them over their shoulders or other body parts. One or more students can disappear under the sheet when they feel brave enough to do so. Use the sheet as you would a parachute; the pillowcase or cloth can be a mini parachute for two students. If you must not make any references to Halloween, you can call this the "Great Parachute Dance" or "parachute play."

The "Giraffe Skip" song has the following routine spoken on the tape:

It's the *giraffe*

Stand up, arms up, hands together

Ready and, step, skip [multiple times].

The music continues after the instructions end. Repeat the step, skip, or add your own movements such as leaning forward, leaning to the side, kneeling down, and standing up.

Verbalize, sign, and introduce the letter. You can recognize colors in students clothing and names that start with G, and ask who is a *girl*.

 **Stations**

Throw, jump, roll and kick, glide, roll, hang, balance, climb

- *Garbage* pickup. Throw pieces of crumpled paper and the like into recycling bins and trash cans.
- Plant a *garden*. Jump high and attach flowers with Velcro to a poster of a garden. After the garden is planted, students can jump high trying to pick all the flowers.
- Score a *goal*. Use the same goals employed for the previous letters for both kicking and rolling, such as boxes, crates, and baskets.
- Gliding. Have the students wear large socks over their shoes, enabling them to *glide* across the floor. A wooden floor works well.
- *Gymnastics*. Logroll and forward roll down an incline. It is easier for children to perform these movements down an incline than on a flat surface.

    Hang on a rope or the parallel bars.

    Walk pieces of "garbage" across the balance beam to a trash can.

    Ask students to put cutouts of both uppercase and lowercase Gs in the correct baskets at the far end of the balance beam.

    Climb on and jump down vaulting boxes, aerobics steps, or low benches (secured against the wall).

    Check to see if you need to do any specific activities related to individual needs.

 **Play Area**

The play area can have gymnastics as a theme. Decorate the area with posters and drawings. Read the "Teaching Tips" related to this area (see figure G1).

 **Closing**

Locomotor Skills Across the Gym. Demonstrate galloping and discuss the commands "ready, set, go." Point out that *go* starts with a G. Besides discussing galloping, allow the students to make choices about the way they want to cross the gym.

Garbage Relay. Reuse the "garbage" from this lesson's station activities and collect it on one end of the gym. Place recycling bins and trash cans on the other end and ask the students to run the garbage to the cans one piece at a time until the whole gym is clean.

Repeat the Friendly Ghost Dance or Great Parachute Dance from the opening.

Repeat the letter, and ask about the words that start with the letter G.

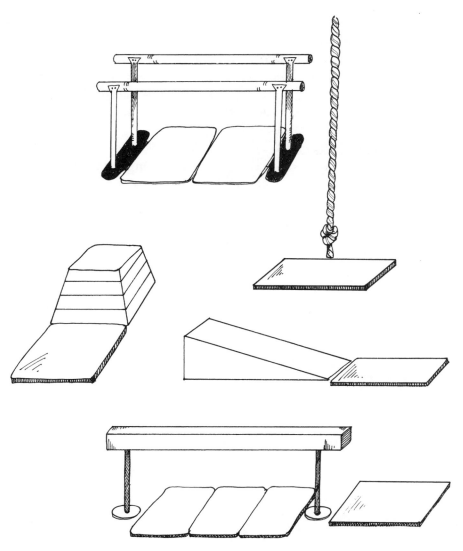

Figure G1   Gymnastics. Mats at each station for safety.

Teaching Tips

- When selecting Halloween music or themes, be aware that not all schools allow activities related to this holiday.
- Be sure you use mats at all your gymnastics stations to keep the activities safe: at the bottom of the incline mat, under the rope and parallel bars, under the balance beam and at the end of the beam where the students jump down, and where the students jump down from the vaulting boxes (see figure G1).
- Depending on the experience of your students, it might be necessary for you to concentrate on the rolling station in gymnastics to ensure proper form. Position yourself in a way that enables you to still see the rest of your space.

- To help students learn the forward roll, have them keep a foam ball under the chin while rolling.
- If you decide to do the back roll as well, a helpful hint is to tell students to "turn your thumbs backward in your ears" to get proper hand placement. Also emphasize pushing off with the hands to finish the roll and take pressure off the head and neck. Again, an incline mat, used under close supervision, can lead to early success.
- Incline mats can be expensive. Make your own by covering a not too large piece of plywood with carpet and raising it a foot on one end. If the piece of plywood is too large, the mat becomes too heavy to move easily.
- Collect old large socks that fit over students' shoes. Ask your colleagues to donate socks, and send a note home with students. Save them for future use.

The Letter H

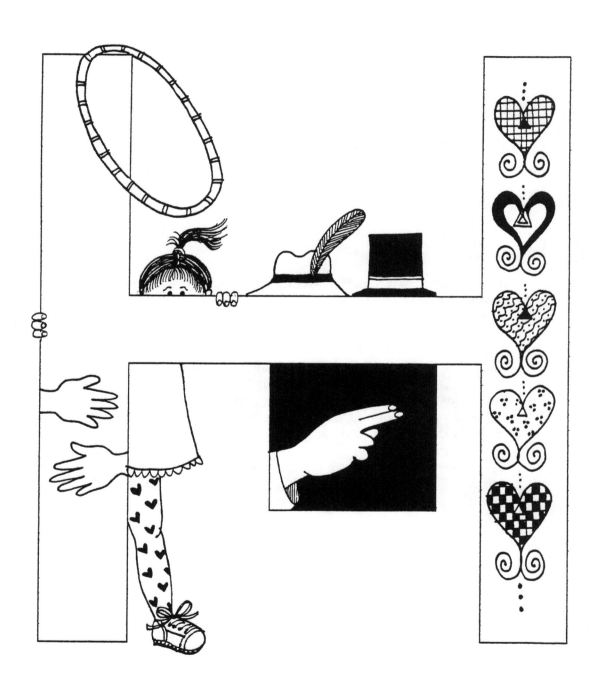

 Words

Body parts: Hair, hand, head, heart(beat), heels

Nouns: Hat, Halloween (represented by orange and black balloons), hoppity-hop, hopscotch, hula hoop

Verbs: Hang, hit, hop

Directions: High

Others: Happy, students' names that begin with H

 Music

Hokey-Pokey. A funky version is available on the CD "Christy Lane's Complete Party Dance Music," available from Human Kinetics. (See Resource D, page 153).

Halloween music (if allowed in your school)

Song: "If You're Happy and You Know It"

 Warm-Up

Try organizing a *hat* day at school, when students can wear hats inside the building all day long and can come to the gym wearing them. Have the gym set up for the regular warm-up routine of jogging or walking laps.

Before the students start their laps, introduce the concept of *heartbeat*. Show the students where they can feel their heartbeat—maybe on the wrist, maybe on the side of the neck, maybe by placing hand over heart. Introduce taking the pulse correctly by using not the thumb but the finger. Ask the students if their pulse is slow or fast. Ask them to say the rhythm out loud: "boom-boom-boom." Follow this with running or jogging laps around the gym. When you give a signal, the students stop and immediately find their heartbeat. Is it faster or slower than before? Continue running, and repeat stopping and feeling the heartbeat a few more times. The easiest place to feel the beat after exercise is to place the hand over the heart. Explain to the students that it is important that your heart can beat faster, and that exercise makes you breathe faster, also. The heart is a muscle the size of a fist, and to make the muscle strong, we have to exercise it.

 Opening

Dance the Hokey-Pokey; it works great in a circle formation. The song has the following lyrics:

Put your right arm in, take your right arm out

Put your right arm in and you shake it all about

You do the Hokey-Pokey and you turn yourself around

That's what it's all about. [Clap when singing this last line.]

Repeat with "left arm," "right foot," "left foot," "right elbow," "left elbow," "head," "bottom," and "whole self."

If it is close to *Halloween* and your school allows activities for this holiday, you can make your own routine and call it the "Witches' Waltz" or "Friendly Ghost Dance" (see "Opening" under the letter G).

"If You're Happy and You Know It." The song has the following lyrics:

If you're *happy* and you know it, clap your hands (2x)

If you're happy and you know it

Then your face will surely show it

If you're happy and you know it, clap your hands.

Repeat, replacing "clap your *hands*" with "pat your *head*," "wave your hand," "comb your *hair*," "click your *heels*," "cross your heart," and so on.

Introduce the letter, discuss the H words already used, sign the letter, and recognize students whose names start with H.

 **Stations**

Push, hit, hop, jump, twist, hang, throw

- Using a broom, push orange and black balloons, foam balls, or beach balls across the gym floor. Add a witch's hat for effect, in case the school does allow Halloween-themed activities. That is also the reason for the colors orange and black for the balloons. (Balls are preferable to balloons because balloons may pop.)
- *Hit* orange and black balloons or balls with your hands or your head.
- Play *hoppity-hop*, also called spring ball or bouncing ball. This is a large ball with a handle. The child sits on the ball straddling the handle. While holding on to the handle, the child bounces on the ball by pushing off with her legs. Listed in any sport catalog.
- Play *hopscotch*.

Hopscotch can be played in a variety of ways, ranging from simple to complex. A simple diagram allows the students to *hop* (on one foot) or jump (on two feet) from square to square until they reach the top. In the top square or circle they turn around and hop or jump back. There are only two simple rules: try not to step on the lines, and hop only once in each square. More advanced students can hop or jump over a square as they go. For example, if you place a beanbag in square one, you have to hop over that square; place the beanbag in square three, and you have to hop over that square. Students who are even more advanced can try to hop or jump part of the diagram backward or on their nonpreferred foot (see figure H1).

- **Hula-Hoop Jumps.** *Hula hoops* are great to use when first introducing jump-rope skills. The student holds the hoop in front, palms down, then steps through the hoop and turns it over the head from back to front. From stepping through, progress to fast stepping as if leaping to jumping with a two-foot takeoff (see figure H2).
- **Hula-Hoop Twists.** Place the hula-hoop around the waist, give it a spin, and keep it going by moving the hips.
- Using your hands, *hang* on a rope, parallel bars, or a chin-up bar.

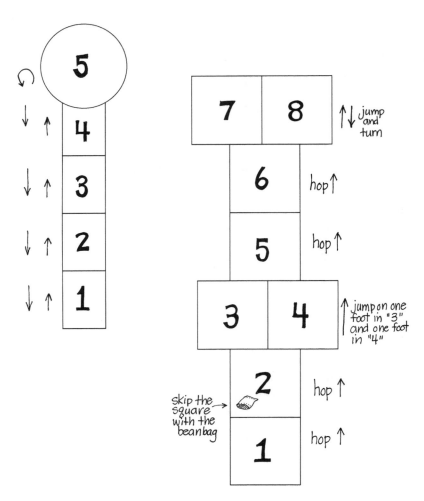

Figure H1 Simple and more complex hopscotch pattern.

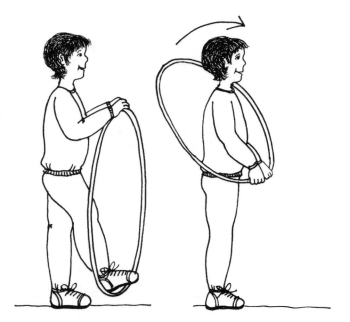

Figure H2 Step and jump through a hula hoop.

- *High* **Jump.** See the station "plant a garden" under the letter G. Other options are taping a yardstick to the wall or hanging a slanted rope between two poles. Ask, "At what point can you still touch the rope when you jump?"
- Throw at targets, using pumpkins or little ghosts as targets to represent Halloween. Or hang cutouts of uppercase and lowercase Hs and invite the students to try to hit only the uppercase or only the lowercase letters.
- Include any activity you need based on students' individual needs.

Play Area

Put the hula-hoop activities and the jumping stations in the play area so that students can practice them at their leisure.

Closing

Organize a fashion parade of students wearing their hats.
Repeat the "Hokey-Pokey" or "If You're Happy and You Know It."

Teaching Tips

- Information on the American Heart Association is included in Resource D.
- When selecting Halloween music or themes, be aware that not all schools allow activities related to this holiday.
- If you are unfamiliar with the songs "Hokey-Pokey" or "If You're Happy and You Know It," ask your school's music teacher or a classroom teacher to sing them for you. Guaranteed, someone will know these classics!
- When talking about heartbeats, do not be concerned with whether students count the heartbeat correctly. If they can, that is great, and you can encourage them; but if not, that is okay too. This introduction to the heart is about the importance and the effect of exercise. Exercise makes the heart muscle work harder; it trains the heart muscle to make it stronger.
- Hang the targets for the throwing station from the basketball rim, from a rope suspended between two volleyball stands, in a hula hoop, in an open doorway, or in any space where you can hang things.
- Make ghosts using Wiffle balls with pieces of white cloth or plastic draped over them. Pull string through the openings in the ball and the top of the cloth to hang the ghosts.
- Use mats for safety when students are hanging on the rope, parallel bars, and monkey bars.
- Draw hopscotch patterns outside using chalk; inside, use masking or floor tape or paint on a long piece of carpet that you can roll out. You can also place hula hoops in a hopscotch pattern and play the game based on the rules you and the students establish. Students can design their own hopscotch patterns.
- Pick up all the pieces of a balloon when it pops, or use balls or beanbags.

The Letter I

 ## Words

Nouns: Ice, ice cream, ice-skating, imagination, island

Verb: Imagine

Directions: In, into, inside

Others: I, students' names that begin with I

 ## Music

To address the question of "What are all the things *I* can do?," sing the song "This Is the Way," to the tune of "The Wheels on the Bus."

Dance the Hokey-Pokey; it mentions the word "in" numerous times.

Play a tape with nature sounds for creative dance using the imagination.

 ## Warm-Up

Scatter *islands* throughout the gym and invite the students to walk all around the area, avoiding the islands and each other. Play nature tapes. When the music stops, the students stand still. When the music plays again, they can start moving again.

The last time you stop the music, explain the idea of creative dance (see "Opening"), and use the scattered formation the students are already in.

 ## Opening

Creative dance: Talk about *imagination*. Ask the students to *imagine* that they are in the scene of the music; for example, on a beach or in a forest. Ask, "What do we see on the beach? Let's close our eyes and imagine we are on the beach. Show me how you walk on the beach in the sand. Now you are stepping in the water. The water feels great, and you go under water and come back up. You make swimming motions with your arms and blow bubbles in the water. The water tastes salty. Walk back on the beach. Dry off with a towel...."

Or for the forest: "You hear the wind blowing, the trees are moving. Show me how the trees are moving. The wind is getting stronger; it starts raining. The rain stops, and the wind calms down. The sun comes out. There are animals in the forest. I see a rabbit. How does the rabbit move? And a snake, how does the snake move? And a deer...."

You can also repeat the Hokey-Pokey and mention the word *in*. (For a description of the dance, see the letter H, page 58.)

Sing "This Is the Way." The first verse is as follows:

This is the way I comb my hair, comb my hair, comb my hair

This is the way I comb my hair, early in the morning.

Add movements, replacing "I comb my hair" with "I stomp my feet," "I wave my hand," "I touch my toes," and so on.

Introduce the letter, sign the letter, and recognize students' names that start with I.

Stations

Throw, kick, balance, jump, skate

- Throw a variety of objects into barrels, buckets, baskets, boxes, and other goals (emphasize *in*, *into*, *inside*).
- Kick balls into goals. Boxes or crates set on their side can be goals.
- Balance a rag ball, table-tennis ball, or any kind of small ball on an *ice cream cone* and walk across a balance beam.
- Designate something as an *island* (poly spot and hula hoop, carpet, vaulting box) and have the students reach the island in a challenging way—for example, walking across a balance beam, planks, or a rope bridge (see figure F1, page 49); or jumping from "stone" to "stone," using carpet squares or hula hoops as stones.
- *Ice-skate* by wearing large socks over the shoes, or use roller skates. Add hats and gloves for effect.
- Add any activity needed based on students' individual needs.

Play Area

The island makes a great center for the play area, with the different ways of getting to the island arranged as spokes around it. Students choose one way to get to the island and another to leave it.

Closing

Upside-Down Ice Cream Cones. Scatter two different kinds of "ice cream cones" across the gym floor, leaving enough room between them for students to move around. Ask stores for their cones or use paper and plastic cups. Divide the class into two groups. The A group is in charge of one type of cone, and the B group is in charge of the other. As long as the music is playing, group A tries to turn all the B cones over, and group B tries to turn all the A cones over. Once the students understand this, add the rule that besides turning over the other group's cones, each group can also set their own cones upright (see figure I1). You can draw an uppercase I on all of group A's cones and a lowercase i on all of group B's.

Island Tag. Scatter "islands" throughout the gym. The islands can be mats or hula hoops. When you are on an island you are safe, and the tagger cannot tag you. To make this game successful for your particular group, you may need to adjust the number of islands, the number of taggers, the distance between the islands, or the time someone is a tagger.

When students are tagged, do not make them leave the game; instead, find ways for them to rotate back in. Very young children do not need a tagger, they

Figure I1 The game Upside-Down Ice Cream Cones.

just love running from one island to the next. They can work on spatial awareness and trying to avoid each other. Once the students understand the basic format, you can add the rule that only one person can be on an island at a time.

Repeat the letter, sign the letter, and recognize words and students' names that start with the letter I. Add an affirmation: "I can." Have the students repeat this affirmation as loudly as they can. At any time during the rest of the year, during any kind of activity, you can ask the children out loud: "Can you [fill in an activity]?" and they answer, "Yes, I can!" or "Yes, I can [activity]!" You might want to post it on the wall for the rest of the school year.

Teaching Tips

- Ask local ice cream stores for their paper cups to use as cones or use paper or plastic cups in two different colors.
- Nature music is available just about everywhere. Look in department stores, music stores, and nature stores.
- Affirmations are powerful tools that can create a positive environment and help students feel good about themselves. You and your students can surely come up with other great affirmations.

The Letter J

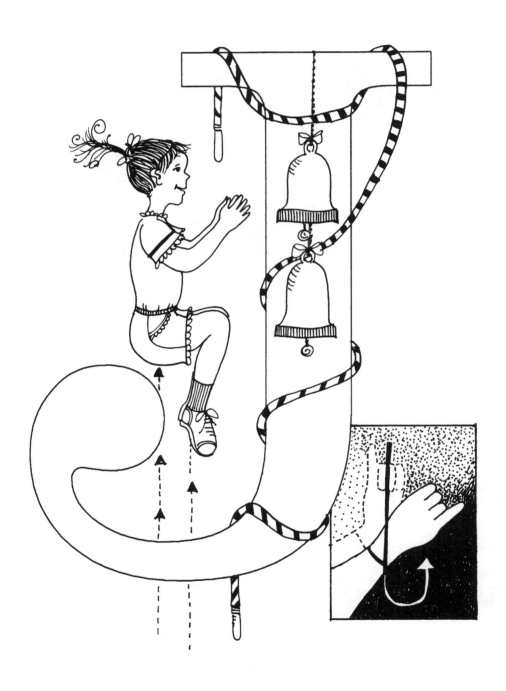

 **Words**

Nouns: Jack-o'-lantern, jail, Jamaica, Japan, jazz, jingle bell, jug, jump rope

Verbs: Jog, juggle, jump

Others: Students' names that begin with J

 Music

Jazz music

Jamaican music (reggae)

Japanese music

"Sittercise" by KIMBO Educational # 2045

 Warm-Up

While *jogging* their laps, have students *jump* over certain areas, such as an imaginary river between two ropes. Have cutouts of the letter J available for those students whose names start with J or for those who want to keep track of how many laps they have jogged.

 Opening

Hand out *jingle bells*, one for each student to put on their shoes. You can repeat the "Sittercise" exercise used for the letter F. This exercise asks for a number of leg and foot motions that emphasize the jingle bells. You can also repeat the guided discovery exercise found under "Opening" for the letter F. Ask the students, "What can you do with your feet?"

You can introduce the students to *jazz* music and design a stretching routine set to the music. See the letter F (flexibility) for stretching suggestions.

Introduce the students to music from *Jamaica* or *Japan*. Perhaps someone born in those countries can come to your gym and introduce music and dancing. This is a great opportunity for integrated curriculum. You or other colleagues can add geographical, social, and cultural information about these countries.

Have the students try some long *jump rope* skills. They line up on one side parallel to the rope and finish on the other side, again parallel to the rope (see figure J1a-b). Invite the students to attempt the following challenges:

Jump over the rope, with one end of the rope low to the ground.

Go under the rope.

Jump over the rope, with the rope moving like a snake.

Jump over the rope, with the rope moving from side to side (as an unfinished turn).

Run under the rope, with the rope fully turned. The students do not touch the rope or jump.

Introduce the letter J. Recognize words that start with the letter, sign the letter, and recognize students whose names starts with the letter J.

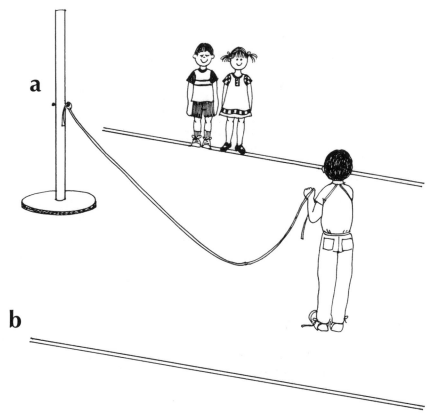

Figure J1   Set up for long jump rope skills.

(a) Hold the rope loosely so it comes undone when a student gets caught.

(b) The line that students start and end behind.

Stations

Jump, throw, catch, juggle

- **Short Jump Rope.** With very young students, adjusting jump rope tricks is necessary. Good substitutions for a regular-size jump rope (which is too long for young children) are a hula-hoop; a jump stick; and a regular-size jump rope cut in half or folded double with the student holding both handles in one hand (see figure J2a-c). The hula hoop and the jump stick encourage practicing stepping or jumping over, followed by turning; the cut rope and the folded rope encourage practicing the rhythm of jumping while turning. Well-selected music can support the jumping rhythm.

- **Long Jump Rope.** See "Opening" for instructions. Indicate where students start, the order in which they go, and where they line up again after they pass the rope. If you used this activity for the opening, the students should know the routine and be able to perform in smaller groups.

- **Standing Long Jump.** Use a marker to write on a roll of carpet, or put down masking tape on the gym floor to indicate the starting point and distance jumped.

- **High Jump.** Hang a rope between two volleyball standards. Make the rope slanted so that everyone can be successful. The objective is to jump up and touch the rope at the highest point possible.

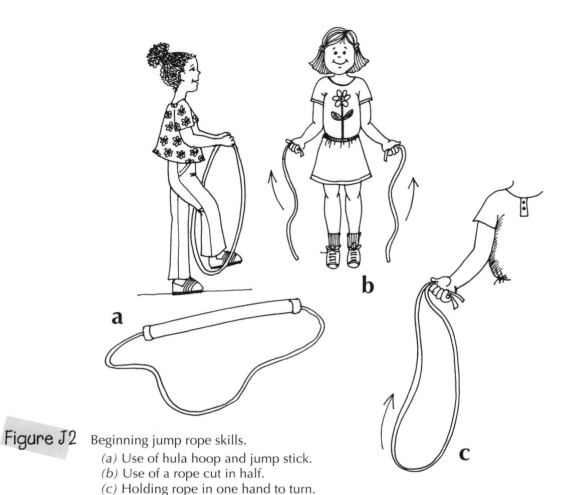

Figure J2   Beginning jump rope skills.
(a) Use of hula hoop and jump stick.
(b) Use of a rope cut in half.
(c) Holding rope in one hand to turn.

- Throwing. Use *jack-o'-lanterns* and jingle bells as targets. You can also distinguish between uppercase and lowercase Js by writing the letters on the targets and instructing students to throw at one or the other.
- **Throw and Catch.** Use scoops made out of milk *jugs* and tennis ball–size balls ("dead" tennis balls, squish balls, or foamballs).
- *Juggling.* Use balls and scarves. Start with one ball or scarf per person. Teach tossing the ball or scarf up in a straight line and catching it before it hits the ground. Start with larger balls, with the students using both hands to throw and catch. Progress to smaller balls or scarves, using only one hand to throw and two hands to catch. Ultimately progress to throwing and catching with one hand.
- Add any activities needed for individual students.

Play Area

Include the repetitive activities of high jump and standing long jump, as well as jumping on the trampoline and down from vaulting boxes. You can repeat favorite activities or activities students need to practice. Keep in mind that the play area requires independent but supervised practice.

Closing

You can repeat the long jump rope routine. Another suggestion is the game **Jump Over the Shoe**. To play, tie a long rope to a heavy object that will not hurt someone whose leg gets hit with it—for example, a shoe. You stand in the middle of the gym, holding the end of the rope that does not have the shoe. Swing the rope around in a circle. You will have to switch hands to prevent the rope from coiling up around you. Keep the rope as low as possible, and invite the students to jump over the rope (see figure J3).

Figure J3   The game Jump Over the Shoe.

Organize a basic tag game with a *jail* and a jailbreak. When students are tagged, they go to "jail"; the jailbreak is needed to let students back in the game. "Jail" can be as simple as a hula hoop on the floor. Another player can run to the "jail" without being tagged and lift the hula hoop up for the "jailbreak." When all players have left the "jail," the hula hoop is put back down, and the game continues.

Another simple way to teach the students the difference between catching and being caught is for you to be the tagger. This role gives you a great, immediate opportunity to direct and help students.

Teaching Tips

- Resource C contains a handout titled "Let's Jump Rope" that you can send home with students. It describes and pictures most of the jump rope activities from this lesson.

- An easy way to attach jingle bells is with twist ties. Another option is ankle bells. Ask your music teacher to donate some bells to your class.

- Try to have at least four different areas where students need to jump during the warm-up. You can have one on each leg of the lap around the gym.

- Jumping rope is an easy activity to practice at home or during recess. Does your facility allow students, teachers, and parents to check out basic pieces of equipment? A handout for practice at home is easy to make. See the example in Resource C.

- The ideal situation for long jump rope practice is four students per rope—two to turn and two to jump. After the first two jumpers have their turn, turners and jumpers trade places.

- Most jump ropes are available in a number of different sizes. You can also order a spool of coiled rope and cut your own lengths. Wrap a piece of masking tape around each end to prevent the rope from unraveling.

- For safety reasons, when students are jumping over a long rope held by others, make sure at least one end of the rope comes undone when a student's foot gets caught on the rope. Drape the rope over the support or over your hand if you are holding the rope. Do not hold the rope tight or tie both ends to the supports. If a student is holding the rope, moving the rope (for the "snake"), or turning the rope, demonstrate that the student needs to let the rope go when someone gets caught.

- When using milk jugs to make scoops, cut out the bottom and the side below the handle; leave the handle.

- For the juggling station, offer choices such as scarves and different-size balls. It sometimes helps to put hula hoops on the floor. The student has to stay inside the hula hoop when throwing and catching.

The Letter K

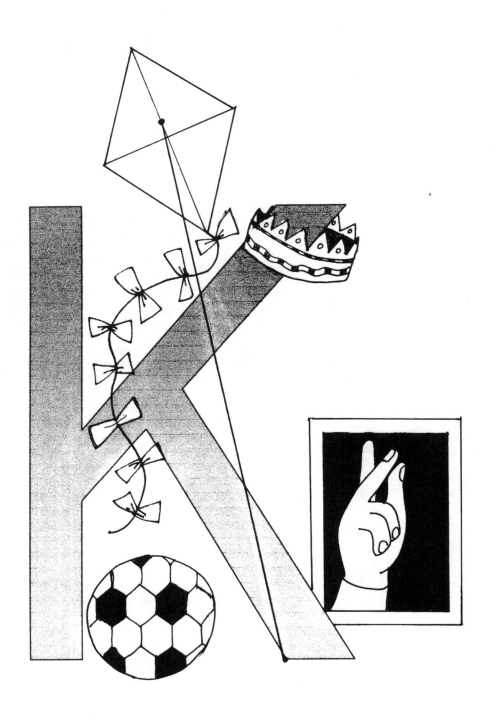

Words

Body parts: Knee
Nouns: Kangaroo, king, kite
Verb: Kick, keep
Others: Students' names that begin with K

Music

Song: "Head, Shoulders, Knees, and Toes"
"Kangaroo Jumps" on the tape "Animal Walks" by KIMBO Educational # 9107

Warm-Up

While doing laps for warm-up, students work on walking or jogging with *knees* up high. The boys can wear paper crowns to be *king* for the day. Explain that boys are kings and girls are queens. The girls will wear crowns for the letter Q.

Opening

Play ***Keep*** **the Ball Going** in circle formation. Students stand with their feet shoulder-width apart. Place a soccer ball in front of a student and ask the student to *kick* the ball to anyone else. This student can then kick it to anyone else, and so on. The object is to keep the ball in the circle. Students need to wait for the ball to roll to them and keep their place in the circle.

Play the song "*Kangaroo* Jumps". The song has the following lyrics:
Here come the kangaroos
Stand tall, bend your knees, hands up
Jump 2, 3, 4, 5, 6, 7, 8 [two times]
Turn 2, 3, 4, 5, 6, 7, 8 [two times]
Jump 2, 3, 4, 5, 6, 7, 8 [two times]
Stand tall, bend your knees, hands up
Get ready to begin again.

Introduce the letter, sign the letter, and recognize words and students' names starting with K.

Stations

Kick, fly a kite, jump

- **Soccer Bowling.** Kick a ball at a target. Targets can be bowling pins, stack of blocks, or cans. Both uppercase and lowercase letters can be introduced here. Write a lowercase k on the lower, smaller targets and an uppercase K on the larger, higher targets.

- **Soccer Scoring.** Kick a ball in a goal. For a goal, use a box, crate, table, or bench set on its side; mark it with two cones; or paint it on the wall.
- Fly a *kite* outside when you have access to a field.
- Kangaroo jumps on the trampoline.
- Add any activity needed for individual students.

Play Area

Suspend balls for students to kick. Put them in a net so that you can hang them from a rope, from the basketball goal, in the doorway, and so on. The kangaroo jumps on the trampoline and students' favorites will round out the play area.

Closing

After the students clean up their last station, they come back to the circle and play Keep the Ball Going from the opening again. Challenge them to break the record. For how many consecutive kicks can they keep the ball(s) in the circle?

Repeat the verbalization of the letter, sign the letter, and recognize the words and names starting with K.

Teaching Tips

- Involve other classes in the school, such as art to make the crowns for the boys to wear.
- The opening game, Keep the Ball Going, can be done sitting on the floor or in chairs, or with some students standing and others sitting.
- Students who cannot use their legs for kicking can hold a hockey stick and push the ball. Choose a ball that is not too heavy and is relatively easy to push.
- Counting can be a motivating factor. When playing Keep the Ball Going, the students can count how many times they (as a group) can kick the ball without the ball rolling outside the circle.
- Making more than one circle for the opening game allows more students to be active at one time.
- To be able to fly kites, you need kites. Ask the classroom staff or the art teacher to help you with this (see figure K1). Building kites is a great cross-disciplinary project. You can also send a handout home to parents describing how to build kites.
- Set a limit when students are jumping on the trampoline—either count or set a timer.
- Allow only one student at a time to jump on the trampoline.
- You can hang a soccer ball in a net on a string between two volleyball standards for students who need to sit while kicking. Make sure the ball is high or low enough for the student to be successful (see figure 9, page 16).

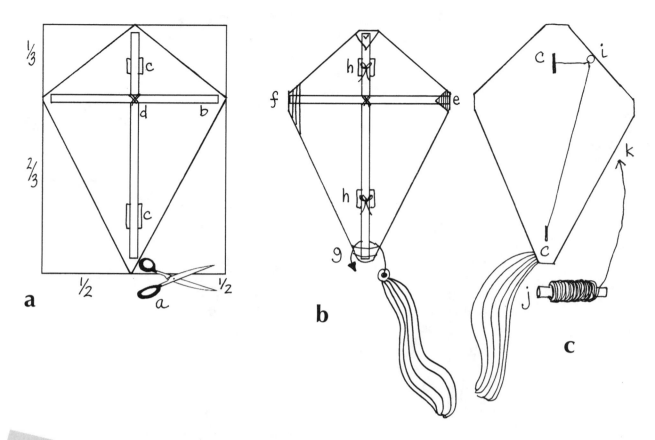

Figure K1 Instructions to build a kite.

    (a) Use a rectangular piece of plastic or kite paper.
        a. Cut the shape of the kite about an 1-1/2 inches wider than the length of the rods indicate.
        b. Lay the rods on the material to make sure it is wide enough.
        c. Place two strips of tape along the midline, making a slit in each from the front.
        d. Tie the rods together, making sure left and right are exactly balanced.

    (b) e. Fold the corners over.
        f. Tape the corners down.
        g. Attach the tail, making sure it is exactly in the middle.
        h. Loop the end of a string through the slit and double-knot it on the rod. The other end of the string goes through the other slit.

    (c) Front of the kite.
        i. Make a loop on the string straight above the top slit.
        j. Wind your twine on a wide piece of wood or tube.
        k. Attach the twine to the loop on the front of the kite.

When flying the kite, keep the string tight. If the kite dives, make the tail heavier to stabilize the kite, or redo the loop on the string, either higher or lower. Also check the balance of the kite. The left and right halves need to be the same.

The Letter L

 ## Words

Body parts: Legs, lungs
Nouns: Ladder, laps, leader, leaves, line, logroll, love, lummi sticks
Verb: Leap
Directions: Left, low, lower
Others: Limbo, loud, students' names that begin with L

 ## Music

Any music good for *limbo* dance. "Limbo Rock" is on the CD "Christy Lane's Complete Party Dance Music."

Instrumental aerobics music to do the activity described in "Opening"

Lummi stick routine (rhythm sticks exercise); KIMBO Educational has a variety of tapes.

Hokey-Pokey (teaches left and right)

 ## Warm-Up

Laps, laps, and more laps, or play Follow the *Leader*. Divide students into small groups and assign each group a leader. Everyone in the group has to follow the leader. The leader has to make sure that everyone can follow, by pacing himself or herself and looking back at times to make sure the group is still together. If not, the leader can stop until everyone is back in line, then continue to move (see the letter F).

You can also draw *lines* on the floor or use existing lines on a gym floor. The students have to follow the lines and stay on them while moving throughout the gym. Design "creeks" for the students to *leap* over. Use mats, jump ropes, or drawn lines to create the creeks.

 ## Opening

Tie a little paper *leaf* to each student's *left* shoe with string, their shoelaces, or twist ties. Now play the aerobics music, emphasizing movements done with the left foot, *leg*, elbow, arm, or hand. Some examples are touch the leaf, lift your left foot, wave with your foot, stamp with your foot, kick your left leg, raise your left arm, and wave with your left hand.

Students can keep the leaves on their shoes throughout the lesson. If you choose to do the Hokey-Pokey (for directions, see the letter H, page 58), the leaf will remind the students which side is their left.

The limbo dance can be done with the whole group or as a station. Have two students hold the rope, or hang it between two volleyball standards or two chairs. Use popular music and challenge the students to go under the rope.

***Lummi Stick* Routine.** If possible, have two sticks for each student; if not, one will do. Demonstrate different ways of tapping (on the floor, on the wall, on a can, on another stick) and different tap rhythms (single taps slow, single taps fast, two taps—rest, etc.). Encourage the students to follow your examples, and have them demonstrate a tap for other students to imitate. Have two signs made, one showing the uppercase L and the other the lowercase l. When you show the uppercase L (the big L), students make big, *loud* sounds. When you show the lowercase l (the small l), they make small, soft sounds.

Talk About Our *Lungs*. Where are they, and what do they do? Are they protected? Ask, "Can you put a lot of air in your lungs? Can you blow all the air out? Can you hold your breath? Put your hand on your chest, on your stomach; do you feel it move? Do we need clean air or dirty air? What makes the air dirty?"

A coloring book from the American Lung Association has the following rhyme:

None of us will ever smoke,

Not even as a silly joke,

And we will do our best each day

To make those cigarettes go away!

Introduce the letter, sign the letter, and recognize words and students' names that start with L.

Stations

Limbo, tap rhythm, jump, crawl, leap, roll, climb

- Limbo dance. See the description under "Opening."
- Lummi stick routine. Make, or ask the music teacher to make, a rhythm tape with very simple rhythms that repeat often and have pauses. If you did not demonstrate the use of the sticks during the opening, do so here. You can also use the tapes from KIMBO Educational. When using this activity as a station, realize that you are not always going to be at that station. The activity has to be simple and must direct itself.
- Put leaves on a tree and take them off. Paint a large, bare tree on a wall in the gym or hang up a paper tree. Put Velcro all over it and have a basket full of laminated leaves, also with Velcro, that stick on the tree. Students must reach, even jump, to reach the top of the tree. Once all the leaves are hung, a storm passes through and all the leaves come down (meaning students reach or jump to take all the leaves off the tree). You can write either uppercase or lowercase Ls on the leaves and ask the students to hang all the uppercase letters in one specific spot and all the lowercase letters in another. You can have two trees for this or different branches in one tree.
- Obstacle course (see figure L1). Set a *ladder* on its side for children to crawl through (make sure it is very stable), arrange carpet squares so that they can leap from square to square, and have mats out for the *logroll*. A logroll is a roll around the vertical axis of the body. Lie down on the mat and make yourself as long as possible. You can even extend your arms over your head. Roll from your back to your stomach to your back, and so forth.

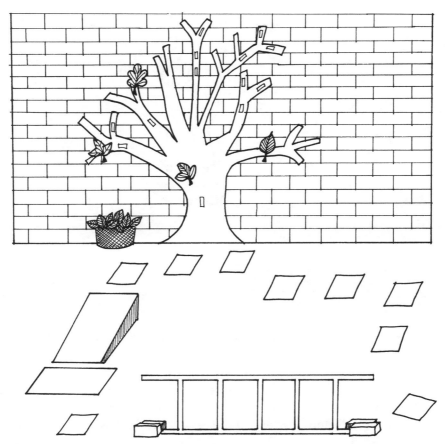

 Figure L1   Obstacle course using the Velcro tree on the wall.

- If you have movable playground-type equipment, you probably have a ladder as part of it, and children can use it to climb.

Play Area

The obstacle course can be the play area; set it up in a circle formation. The students can choose which challenges they want to do.

 ## Closing

Leaf Relay. Drop as many leaves as you can find all over the gym floor Ask the students to help you clean them up by putting them in a basket. The students can bring only one leaf at a time until all the leaves are in the basket. If you use the leaves marked uppercase or lowercase L (see station on putting leaves on a tree), you can have two baskets ready, one for uppercase and one for lowercase.

You can also repeat an activity from the opening section such as Follow the Leader or the Hokey-Pokey.

Teach the sign for "I *love* you" (see figure L2).

Repeat signing and verbalizing the letter; recognize words and students' names that begin with L.

Figure L.2   Sign language sign for "I love you."

 Teaching Tips

- Information on the American Lung Association can be found in Resource D.

- In Follow the Leader, be a leader yourself and demonstrate different locomotor movements and arm movements that your group has to follow. This will give the student leaders ideas and allow them to be creative as well. Rotate leaders so that every student is the leader once.

- While following the lines in the warm-up, students will end up facing each other and needing to pass. You can designate the way they pass. For example, one student lies down and the other student steps over him or her, or one student spreads the legs and the other student crawls through.

- For the limbo dance, when you hang the rope between two standards you have the option to hang it higher on one end and *lower* on the other.

- You need quite a number of leaves for this lesson. Ask adult volunteers and older students to help cut them out of paper that has been laminated. Using laminated paper helps preserve the leaves for many years to come.

The Letter M

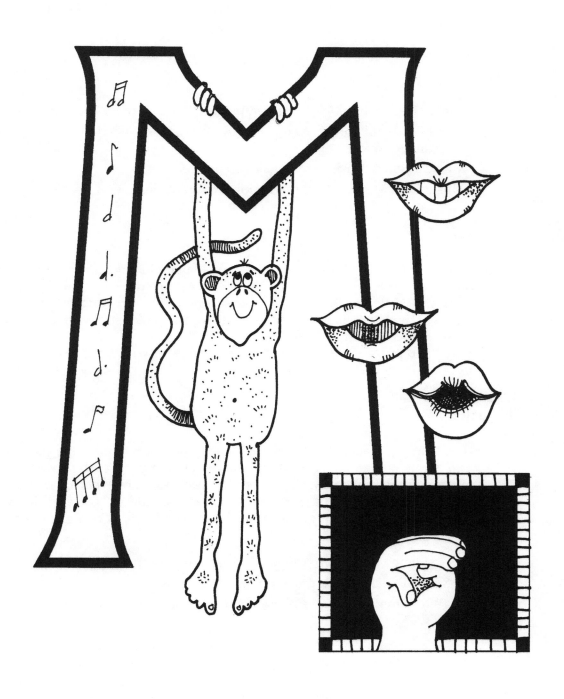

Words

Body parts: Mouth

Nouns: Mat, mattress (air mattress), maze, monkey, music, Mexico

Verbs: March, move, melt

Others: Metro (the name of my school), mmmmmmm (humming), students' names that begin with M

Music

Song: "Head, Shoulders, Knees, and Toes." The word *mouth* is in the lyrics.

Marching band music. Many John Philip Sousa marches are available on recordings.

Musical chairs music. Any music can be used.

Music from Mexico. Ask international clubs, colleagues, or parents.

Warm-Up

Students walk or jog laps around the gym. Play marching band *music* and invite your students to *march* along with the music. As they do so they can pretend they are playing different instruments such as the flute, horn, and big drum. Have cutouts of the letter available for students whose names start with the M or who need the cutouts to stay on task.

My hand puppet, a *monkey*, visits class and stays with me the whole day. The puppet's name is Orly.

Opening

When singing "Head, Shoulders, Knees, and Toes," point out to the students that *mouth* starts with an M. A great variation is to hum parts of the song while still performing the movements. The first time around, hum every time you would sing "head"; the second time, hum all the "head, shoulders" parts. Each time you go through the whole song, add the next word to the parts being hummed. This is what it sounds like:

> First time: "*Mmmmm,* shoulders, knees, and toes…"
>
> Second time: "Mmmmm, mmmmm, knees, and toes…"
>
> Third time: "Mmmmm, mmmmm, mmmmm, and toes, mmmmm, and toes…"

Continue until you end up humming the whole song.

To play musical chairs, you can use the marching band music from the warm-up or other upbeat popular music. You can use real chairs or substitute carpet squares, hula hoops, poly spots, or pieces of tape on the floor.

Because my school's name starts with an M (for *Metro*), we do a cheer and use pom-poms.

During all these activities my hand-puppet monkey participates and is really the one talking to the students instead of me.

Invite someone from *Mexico* to share music and dance with your students.

Students verbalize and sign the letter. Recognize words and students' names that start with M.

Stations

Jump, roll, walk, throw

- The most popular station is the *mattress* (air mattress). Invite the students to perform the following movements: walk, jump, jump–fall on your knees–jump back up, jump–sit down–jump back up, jump and turn, and logroll. Watch your students; they will come up with many more ideas.
- Walk through a *maze* (see figure M1a-b). Use yarn to make a maze on the floor. There is only one way to get to the finish if the lines of the maze are

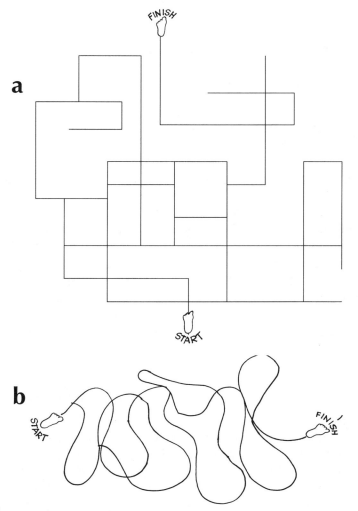

Figure M1   Maze.

(a) Using straight lines and tape on the floor.

(b) Using rope and yarn, resulting in curvy lines.

followed. You can set up two mazes—one for uppercase M and one for lowercase. You can also overlap these two mazes and possibly do them in two different colors.

- Roll on incline *mats*. Practice the logroll, the forward roll, and maybe, with your help, the backward roll (see gymnastics under the letter G, page 54).
- Make music. Hang cowbells on a rope between two standards, in a hula hoop, or from the basketball goal. Throw a ball against the bells to make them ring.
- **Create a Tune.** Tape a piece of enlarged music paper to the wall at the end of an obstacle course. Ask the students to follow the obstacle course, and each time they come to the paper to write a musical note on it. Explain that they can draw the dots anywhere on the lines, from left to right. At the end of class, play the created tune on an instrument.
- Add any activities that needed repeating or to meet the needs of individual students.

Play Area

The air mattress and incline mats stations can be your play area, if you have enough mats to be secure. Otherwise the maze is a great self-repeating station, students can try this over and over again without teacher direction.

Closing

Use slow music for a cool-down. Ask the students to *melt* to the floor, where they relax following your directions. Suggest that they close their eyes, feel their breathing go in and out, and breathe in deep. A basic relaxation technique is to tense a muscle, then completely relax it. To introduce this technique, ask the students to point their toes, and relax; stretch their fingers, and relax; shrug their shoulders, and relax; feel tall, and relax.

You can also repeat the stretching exercises described as a closing activity under the letter F (see page 50). If you need a more energetic closing, use any of the suggestions from "Opening."

Teaching Tips

- Consider bringing in a stuffed animal or hand puppet, and relate its name or species to one of the letters. Younger children respond very well to these animals.
- When playing musical chairs, please do not eliminate anyone from the game. With this age group, simply changing positions, working on listening to the beat of the music, and paying attention to when the music stops is more than enough fun and keeps everyone moving.
- Your school's name probably does not start with M. Make up a cheer for your school and use it during the appropriate letter lesson. An activity like this is great for encouraging school spirit.

- When students are jumping on the air mattress, keep a close eye on safety. The following rules are a must: Have children take their shoes off and place them in a designated space. Limit the number of students jumping at one time. When there are students waiting, use a timer and set it for a few minutes. Place mats around the air mattress in case a student jumps too far or rolls off the mattress. When suggesting the logroll, do not allow any jumping at the same time.

- It is best to have students walk through the maze. They cannot pass each other unless they have turned around to try another way.

- The easiest way to make the maze is to put down the correct path first with a long piece of yarn or rope. After that you can tape down the other long pieces any way you want.

Words

Body parts: Nose

Nouns: Name, net, Newcombe, newspaper, noise

Direction: North, northeast

Others: Next, nine, not, students' names that begin with N

Music

Song: "Head, Shoulders, Knees, and Toes." The word *nose* is part of the lyrics.

Any previously used and therefore familiar tapes, to be used at the beginning of the opening.

Warm-Up

Play **Which Way?.** Tape the four wind directions on the four sides of your space. Invite the students to go *north*, to go south, to go opposite of south, to go to the left, to go to the right, to go to the *next*, to go *northeast*, and so on (see figure N1).

And of course, have children walk or jog laps around the gym. Have cutouts of the letter N available for those students whose *names* begin with N and for those who want to count their laps.

Opening

Use the familiar exercise music to get the students going; for example, one of the tapes with instructions spoken on the tape. Then turn the music off and explain that *nine* starts with the letter N, and the group is going to do all the exercises nine times—nine jumps, nine leg kicks, and so on. This is most easily accomplished by *not* using recorded music. Recorded music has four or eight beats, and nine movements do not fit the rhythm.

Sing the song "Head, Shoulders, Knees, and Toes," and point out that *nose* starts with N. You can paint the students' noses red, like a clown's nose.

The students verbalize and sign the letter. Recognize words and students' names that start with N.

Stations

Jump, roll, balance, crawl, throw, bat, catch

- Use the four wind directions from the warm-up. Underneath each sign indicating N, E, S, or W, post a drawing of an exercise. Suggested exercises are jumping rope, rolling down an incline, walking on cans (see the letter F), and walking across a balance beam. Place a stack of cards, upside-down, in the middle of the gym. The cards have an N, E, S, or W written on them. Each student draws a card, looks at it, and goes to the wind direction written on the card to do the exercise posted there. When finished, the

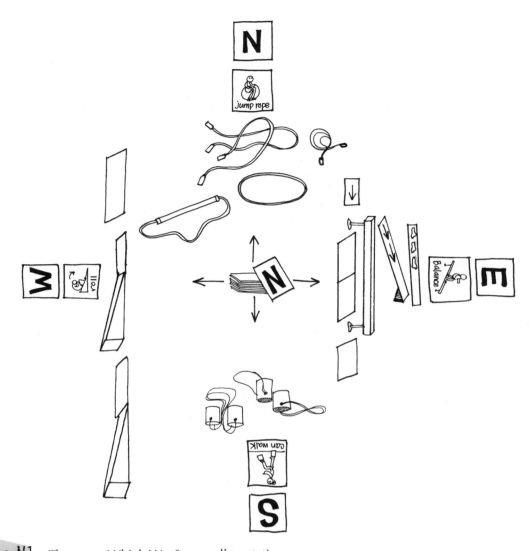

Figure N1   The game Which Way?, as well as stations.
   In order: Jump rope at the N, balance at the E, can walking at the S, rolling at the W.

student runs back to the middle of the gym, puts his or her card back in the stack, and draws another.

It is easy to add the lowercase letters of n, e, s, and w. Place these signs next to the uppercase signs. Also make additional cards with the lowercase letters for the stack of cards. Students can do the same exercises for both the upper- and lowercase letter, or you can add exercises for the lowercase letters.

- **Newspaper Crawl-Through.** Tear out the inside of a sheet of *newspaper* and have students crawl through the remaining border as part of a short obstacle course. Emphasize the word next.

- Throw foam balls at someone holding up a newspaper. The students love it when this person is one of the teachers. Foam balls do not hurt, and they make a lot of *noise* when they hit the paper.

- Set up batting activities such as batting a balloon, beach ball, or foam ball with the hand or with a racket, counting to nine.

- *Newcombe.* Set up a volleyball-type situation. The students throw and catch a balloon, beach ball, or foam ball across the *net*. The object of the game is to keep the ball from touching the floor.
- Add any activities related to students' individual needs.

Play Area

Make a newspaper. Have blank pieces of paper on the wall and markers, crayons, stickers, pictures, and the like available. Invite the students to write or draw a newspaper about the important things in their lives.

Closing

Recycling Race. Place pieces of newspaper all over the gym and invite the students to help put all the paper in the recycling bins. Everyone runs back and forth carrying only one piece of paper at a time until all the paper is cleaned up. Repeat verbalizing and signing the letter. Recognize words and students' names that start with N.

Teaching Tips

- For the stations related to the wind directions you can use any exercise or station from previous lessons. This will give the students an extra opportunity to practice, and you do not have to explain something new.
- Start collecting newspapers a week in advance of this lesson, and ask colleagues to bring in their newspapers too. You can reuse most papers from one class to the next.
- Laminate the signs for the wind directions as well as the cards. Once you get the materials ready, they will serve you many more times.
- Children are supposed to crawl through the newspaper gently, without tearing the paper, but just in case, have a few extra papers ready.
- Instead of foam balls you can use homemade snowballs. Crumple up about half a sheet of newspaper and put it in a small plastic sandwich bag.
- Make up the rules for newcombe as needed. Can a student catch the ball more than once before it goes back over the net? Do you want to count how many consecutive good catches students make, from both sides together? Do you want to add sidelines and a baseline so that the ball can be out? All these are suggestions; rules are based on the situation and ability.
- Set up multiple newcombe situations to keep the groups small. You can use volleyball nets, badminton nets, ropes, or even a table or a row of chairs. The groups can be as small as one on one.
- Be alert when using balloons, because pieces of popped balloons present a choking hazard. When possible use alternatives such as beach balls or foam balls.

The Letter O

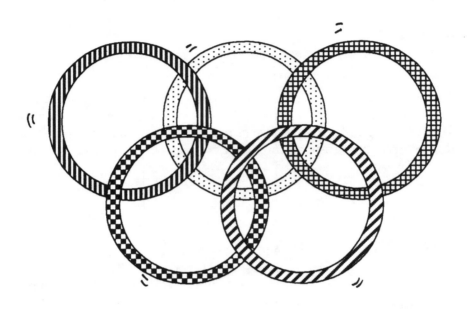

Words

Color: Orange

Nouns: Obstacle course, Olympics, ostrich

Directions: On, over

Others: Orly (my hand puppet returns!), shapes of the letter O (hula hoops, deck tennis rings), students' names that begin with O

Music

"Ostrich Strut" from "Animal Walks" by KIMBO #9107

Any movement that can be done in a circle formation, such as the square dance (see letter D), the Hokey-Pokey (see the letter H), beanbag song (see the letter B), and "Aerobics USA" (see "Music" under the letter A, page 22).

Warm-Up

While walking or jogging their assigned laps, students face *obstacles* they have to go *over*. Suggestions for obstacles include a rope hanging between poles, a rope taped over the top of two cones, a stick on two cones, low hurdles, and gym mats. Use *orange* arrows, tape, or yarn to indicate in which order the obstacles are to be taken.

Opening

The "Ostrich Strut" song contains the following words and associated movements:

This is the *ostrich*

Stand tall, hands on hips

Elbows out

Pick your knees up

Walk, 2, 3, 4, 5, 6, 7, 8

Bend over, keep your legs straight

Put your head down, and again.

You can repeat any of the circle formation activities described under "Music." Point out the circle (the O shape) to the students. You can emphasize this by having the students stand in hula hoops. To introduce the letter show the poster, verbalize and sign the letter, and recognize words and students' names that start with O.

In my classes, *Orly* the hand puppet comes back and participates as much as possible.

 Stations

Throw, bat, jump/leap, climb, Olympics

- Hang hula hoops to throw balls through.
- Hang orange balloons or balls, which are preferred, and bat them with a badminton racket or the hand.
- Make a path with hula hoops on the floor for students to follow. You can add the obstacles used in the warm-up to this station to repeat the concept of over.
- Hopscotch using hula hoops. Students can step, leap, hop, or jump the hopscotch pattern they create.
- Climb *on* and over vaulting boxes.
- **Ring Toss.** Use bowling pins, blocks, plastic soda bottles, or similar objects as pins. Throw deck tennis rings and hula hoops.
- Add any activity related to individual objectives.

Summer Olympics: Jump, throw, catch, cycle, dribble, kick

- **Standing Long Jump.** Use a marker to write on a roll of carpet or put tape on the floor to indicate starting point and distance jumped (see under "Stations" for the letter J).
- **High Jump.** Hang a rope between two standards. Slant the rope so that everyone can be successful (see under "Stations" for the letter J, page 68).
- **Throwing for Distance.** Have the students throw at a wall from a set distance. Ask, "Who can make it to the wall?"
- **Newcombe.** Repeat from "Stations" for the letter N. Set up a volleyball situation using a balloon, beach ball, or foam ball. Invite the students to throw (and catch) the ball back and forth over the net. The ball cannot touch the floor.
- **Cycling.** Students can do this on tricycles, stationary bikes, and the like.
- **Soccer.** See the activity under "Stations" for the letter D (dribble on page 39) and for the letter K (kick on page 73).
- **Basketball.** See the "Stations" activity for the letter D (dribble). Introduce shooting on a goal if you have low goals. Use smaller balls so that the students can be successful.

Winter Olympics: Glide, skate, ski, push

- **Gliding.** Students put oversized socks over their shoes.
- **Skating.** Students use roller skates or in-line skates.
- **Skiing.** Cross-country skis would be great. An alternative is homemade skis—pieces of wood approximately one foot long with Velcro straps to put your feet in or shoeboxes can be used. Only the front of the foot is strapped in; the heel can come up from the board when taking a step.
- **Pushing.** Use a scooter board like a luge, pushing it with the feet. Ask, "See how far you can roll on one push . . . on two pushes . . . on many pushes as in a sprint before you lift your feet up and roll."

Play Area

This area can have the summer games as a theme. Selected activities are jumping, basketball shooting, and suspended soccer balls. Decorate the area with posters, a welcome sign, the *Olympic* rings, and the like. Or you can simply use the stations and include batting and the obstacle course when you do not choose the Olympic theme.

Closing

You can repeat the circle activities from the opening.

Play **Don't Break the Circle**. The students form a circle by holding hands. Around the arm of one student is a large hula hoop or a rope with ends tied together to form a circle. The object of the activity is for the students to pass the hula hoop or rope around the circle without anyone letting go of the hands. Students can help each other, but they have to hold hands at all times.

Teaching Tips

- There is no activity to distinguish between uppercase O and lowercase o because the shapes are exactly the same.

- Keep the obstacles low during the warm-up so that everyone can be successful. Students who use wheelchairs can go over the obstacles (such as a mat) where possible, or they can go around.

- Make sure you pick up the pieces of the balloons when they pop because they present a choking hazard. Beach balls and foam balls are preferred.

- Remember to use rackets with short handles.

- When throwing for distance, make sure the students all stand behind a line before they throw and wait until you tell them it is clear before they go to retrieve their balls.

- For newcombe teaching tips, see under the letter N.

- Toy stores sell low basketball goals. Sometimes you can find one that fits over a door. Or make your own by taping or screwing a basket with the bottom cut out onto the wall.

- For roller-skating practice, roll out pieces of carpet for students to skate on if they do not trust themselves to go on the regular floor yet. Skating on carpet is slower, and it acts as a buffer when children fall.

- To make it easier to put skates on and take them off, replace the buckle or clasp on the ankle strap with Velcro (see page 15).

- Fisher-Price roller skates let you lock the rear wheels or make them only go forward.

- At the skiing station, have short canes available to help students with balance if needed.

- When playing Don't Break the Circle, first demonstrate in a large circle. Then break up into small circles, or have more than one rope going at a time. This will increase active participation time.

- If you choose to use the Olympic theme, have certificates of participation available for students to take home (see figure O1).

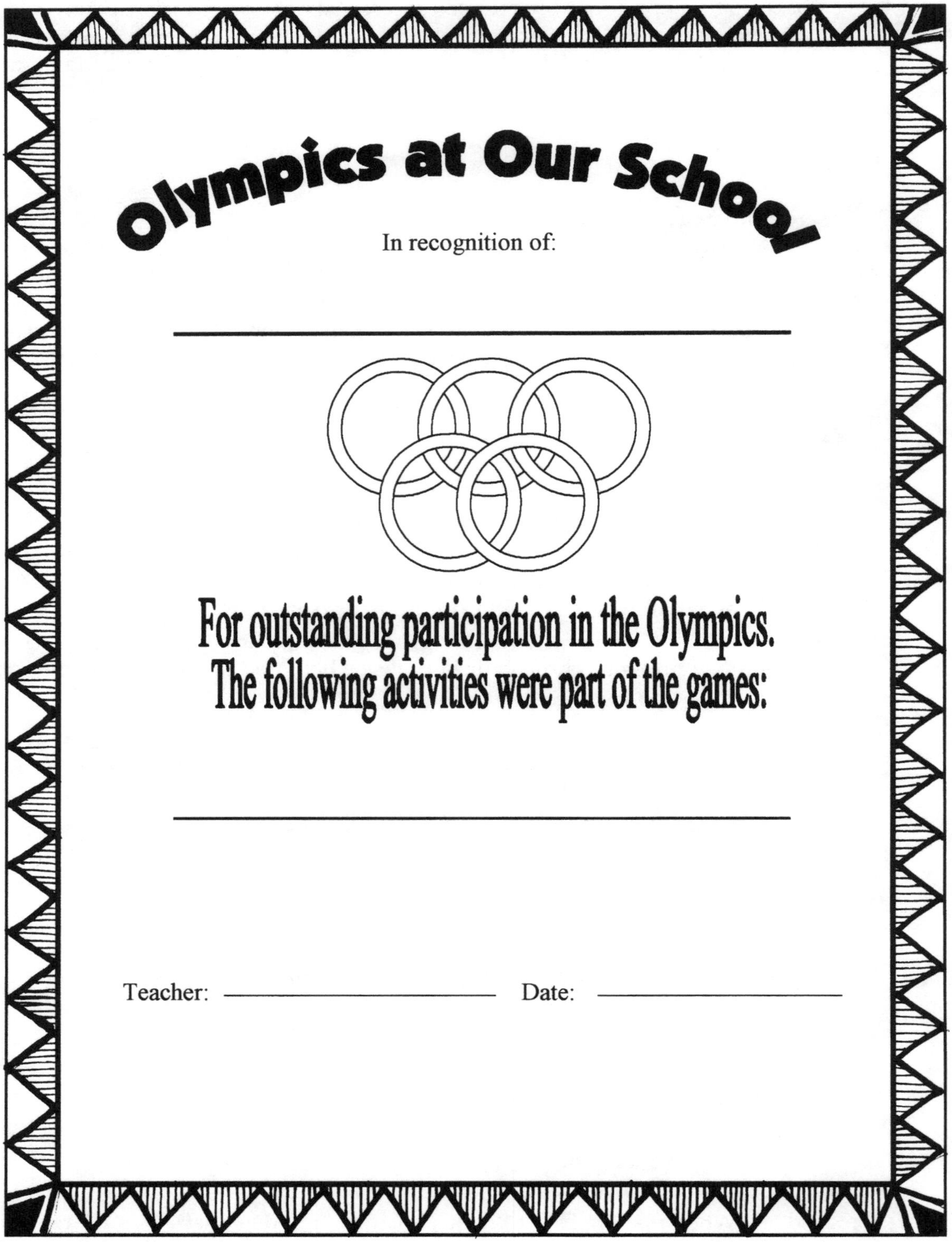

Olympics at Our School

In recognition of:

_____

**For outstanding participation in the Olympics.
The following activities were part of the games:**

_____

Teacher: _____   Date: _____

Figure O1   Certificate of participation in the Olympics.

The Letter P

 Words

Color: Purple

Nouns: Parachute, partner, pat, penguin, percussion, physical education (PE), push-ups, patty-cake, pathways

Verbs: Play, pick, pull, push

Others: Students' names that begin with P

 Music

"Penguin Shuffle" from "Animal Walks" by KIMBO #9107

Song: "Hand Rag" on the tape "Hand Jivin'" by Educational Activities Inc.

Percussion, either by using percussion instruments or a recording such as the Broadway show "Stomp"

 Warm-Up

Play a tape with *percussion* music, or hand out percussion instruments while inviting everyone to walk or march to the beat. Instruments can be homemade or borrowed from the music teacher. Lummi sticks (rhythm sticks) can be used here, as well as tambourines, drums, and so on. You can use *purple* arrows or yarn to make *pathways*. Have cutouts of the letter P available for students whose names start with P or for those who need or want them to count their laps.

 Opening

The song "Penguin Shuffle" has the following words and movements:

Here come the *penguins*

Stand tall, toes out

Arms straight, hands up

Now walk. [You can add movements for going sideways and backward, leaning forward to eat, and flapping your hands to swim.]

The song "Hand Rag" is a *partner* exercise, and it asks students to shake hands (left, right, and both), play *patty-cake*, hold hands, and so on.

Demonstrate *push-ups*. Do wall push-ups, modified push-ups, and regular push-ups, and have the students follow you. Talk about the muscles involved, such as the chest and the triceps.

Parachute play can be done with the whole group. Invite the students to try some of the following activities. Hold the parachute by its handles and move it up and down slowly, with all students moving up and down at the same time.

Walk to the left, walk to the right (in a circle).

Have students go under the parachute, one at a time, when you call their names.

Keep one or more balls on the parachute.

KIMBO Educational has tapes available for parachute games, and numerous activity books are available that include ideas for parachute play.

Students sign and verbalize the letter and recognize words and students' names that start with P. Be sure to mention *physical education*!

 ## Stations

Parachute, bat, pull, throw, catch, push, play

- Use parachute activities as described under "Opening," in smaller groups.
- Bat suspended or free-floating purple balloons with a badminton racket or the hand. Foam balls or beanbags are highly recommended as alternatives to balloons.
- *Pull* a wagon or scooter board with a partner (another student) on it holding a rope.
- Throw and catch a ball with a partner.
- *Push* a ball using a broom or hockey stick. Students can do this moving around freely or following a set path. The path can lead to a goal.
- Add any activity needed to meet individual goals and objectives.

 ## Play Area

Set up a purple play area using purple balls, beanbags, or balloons for batting; purple ribbons in hula hoops for targets; and purple shakers for percussion music. Add favorite stations as needed.

 ## Closing

Repeat the percussion music from the opening, or use the push a ball activity found under "Stations" as a relay.

Pick the Pin Flowers. Use clothespins marked with different colors as "pin flowers." Written on each pin is an uppercase or lowercase P. Drop the pins on one end of the gym floor and ask the students to go and *"pick"* them (one at a time) and put them in a basket or vase. Have one container for the uppercase letters and one for the lowercase. In addition to distinguishing between uppercase and lowercase, students can be asked to distinguish between the different-colored "flowers."

 ## Teaching Tips

- When inviting students to walk to the beat of the percussion music or to play the music, realize that each student has his or her own beat, and it will not be perfect.
- You can make percussion instruments out of anything (see figure P1a-f). When using the rhythm sticks students can tap on the floor, on another stick, on a can, and so on. You can make your own shakers by putting beans

inside a toilet paper roll and covering the ends of the roll or by putting beans, beads, or marbles in a can with a lid (see figure P1a-f).

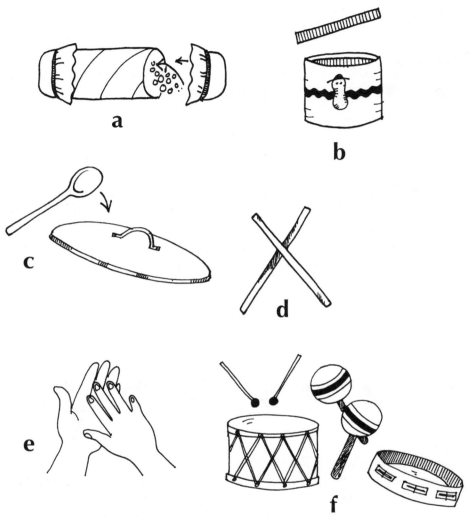

Figure P1   Percussion instruments.

(a) Made from a toilet paper roll with beans or beads inside.
(b) Made from a can with beans, beads, or marbles inside.
(c) A lid and a spoon.
(d) Two sticks.
(e) Clap hands.
(f) Commercial percussion instruments (drum, shakers, tambourine).

- If you do not have a parachute, you can substitute a flat sheet. This might not be large enough for the whole class, so you will need more than one sheet, or you can use this activity as a station.

- Please pick up the pieces of popped balloons, as the pieces present a choking hazard. For batting, use rackets with short handles.

- Make it clear that when pulling a partner in a wagon or on a scooter board, students must only walk, not run. The purpose is to provide a nice, safe ride.

The Letter Q

Aa: Words

Body part: Quads (quadriceps)
Nouns: Queen, question, question mark
Others: Quack, quickly, quiet, students' names that begin with Q

Music

Song: "Old McDonald Had a Farm" (the duck says *quack*)

Warm-Up

As soon as the students enter the gym, introduce the letter by asking them who can do the warm-up as *quietly* as possible. Everyone uses a whisper voice throughout the whole lesson. This facilitates the students being as quiet as possible. The students also walk on tiptoes where possible. Have cutouts of the letter Q available for students whose names begin with Q and for those who want to count their laps.

Opening

Ask students to move quietly. Say to them, "Quietly we do our exercises. We strengthen our *quads* by bending our knees, almost squatting down, holding it for a few seconds, and standing back up." Add other exercises the group has done in the past such as push-ups, jumping jacks, and arm circles. Ask the students for suggestions.

Ask students to move *quickly*. Challenge them to sit down quickly, stand up quickly, turn around quickly, run to the other side of the gym quickly, and so on. Add the opposite of quickly: slowly. Walk across the gym slowly, skip slowly, and so on.

Ask *questions*. Make a poster of a *question mark*. Hold the poster up while putting the previously mentioned opening activities in question form: "Can we bend our knees? Can you show me three push-ups? Can we run to the other side quickly? Who can skip very slowly?"

Sing "Old McDonald Had a Farm." Add movements by singing, "On that farm he has a walking duck, a diving duck, a flying duck."

Ask the question, "Who can be a *queen*?" The girls and female teachers can be queens. They can wear crowns throughout the lesson. (Remember, the boys had their turn earlier to be kings.)

Have the students sign and verbalize the letter. Recognize words and students' names that start with Q.

Stations

Balance, tumble, climb, leap

- Offer the balance stations described in previous lessons, but now students walk quietly on their tiptoes (see figure Q1).

Figure Q1 Trying to be quiet by walking on tiptoes.

- Include any previously offered activity that can be done quietly: tumbling on the mat, climbing on the vaulting box, and the like.
- Leaping across carpet squares (or other easy obstacles) done quickly. This is a great station for adding uppercase and lowercase letters. Ask each student to take along a letter and drop it in the correct basket.
- Use any of the closing activities from previous lessons done quickly: Apple Race (letter A, page 24), It's Raining Balls (B, page 28), Egg Clean-Up (E, page 44), Garbage Relay (G, page 54), Upside-Down Ice Cream Cones (I, page 64), Leaf Relay (L, page 79), and Recycling Race (N, page 89).
- Add any activity to meet individual needs.

 ## Play Area

Select favorites from previous letters and keep emphasizing doing things quietly.

 ## Closing

Play All Ears, found under "Closing" for the letter E. Stretching and relaxation also make for a great quiet activity. See under "Closing" for the letters F and M for specific stretches and relaxation exercises.

 ## Teaching Tips

- Make a handout with exercises on it for students to take home. Use clear pictures that demonstrate proper form and the correct names for muscle groups and exercises.

- Ask your art teacher, volunteers, or older students to help make crowns. Or you can make them yourself from wide strips of paper.
- A great setup to repeat the relays quickly is to do them all at once, with the students puting the objects in the correct places—apples in the basket, eggs in the carton, garbage in a trash can, leaves in a leaf bag, newspapers in a recycling bin. When they finish, simply throw it all out on the floor again and start over.

The Letter R

 Words

Color: Red

Nouns: Raccoon, race, racket, ring, rabbit, rat, rattlesnake, rooster

Verbs: Reach, relax, rest, rock 'n' roll, roll, run

Directions: Right

Others: Ready-set-go, students' names that begin with R

 Music

"Raccoon Rock" from "Animal Walks" by KIMBO #9107

Rock 'n' roll music

Hokey-Pokey (mentions right and left)

Upbeat aerobics music

Relaxation tapes, such as those from Ellipsis Arts, or nature sounds

 Warm-Up

Use *red* arrows, yarn, or tape to mark where the students need to *run* for the warm-up. You can play *rock 'n' roll* music. Have cutouts of the letter R available for students whose name starts with R and those who want to count their laps.

 Opening

Play the rock 'n' roll music, and teach your students by demonstrating how to twist (it is great fun). See the suggestions mentioned under "Opening" for the letter D on page 37. You can add a game to this free dancing by playing Freeze (see the letter D, page 39).

> The song "Raccoon Rock" has the following lyrics and movements spoken on the tape:
>
> Here comes the *raccoon*
>
> Hands on the floor
>
> Walk 2, 3, 4, rock 2, 3, 4 [repeat two more times]
>
> Stop, and start again.

This song leaves plenty of room to be creative. Add the movements of other animals to this song. Some suggestions are a *rabbit* that hops, a *rat* that scurries, a *rattlesnake* that slithers, and a *rooster* that prances.

Tie a red *ribbon* or string to each student's *right* foot. A red dot (using a marker or a sticker) can work, too. Use the upbeat aerobics music, and ask the students to perform movements with their right side—for example, touch the red ribbon, shake your right foot, kick with your right foot, wave your right hand, circle with your right arm, and so on.

When students are performing the Hokey-Pokey, the red ribbon reminds the students which side is their right side. For instructions for the Hokey-Pokey, see under "Opening" for the letter H.

To introduce the letter, point out red in everyone's clothes and emphasize *remembering* which foot is the right foot. Sign and verbalize the letter, and recognize words and students' names that start with R.

Stations

Bat/strike, kick, reach, rock, roll

- Use *rackets* to bat or strike (with the right or left hand) suspended red foam balls or beanbags. Balloons may be used under close supervision. Challenge students to bat or strike free-floating balls or balloons.
- Kicking activities using the right or left foot. See the activities outlined under the letter K for kicking, the letter D for dribbling, and the letter I for in(to).
- *Reach* to hang red valentines (hearts) in a tree painted on the wall. After all the hearts are on the tree, reach to take them all down. Challenge the students to hang all hearts with a lowercase r on one side of the tree and all hearts with an uppercase R on the other side.
- Create rocking boards and other balancing boards (see figure R1).

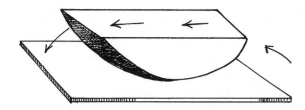

footprints
balance left to right

footprints
balance back to front

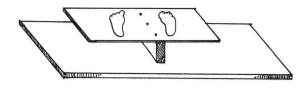

Figure R1 Homemade rocking boards.

- Practice *rolling*—logroll, forward roll, and backward roll. Use incline mats if you have them.
- Add any activity related to individual objectives.

Play Area

Rocking boards are a source of endless entertainment. You can include the tree and possibly the batting station. Watch out for swinging rackets; using the hands to bat the red balls is safer.

Closing

Invite the students to *relax* by lying down on the floor on their backs while you play relaxing music. Ask them to close their eyes while *resting*. You can mention breathing in and out slowly, arms and legs feeling heavy, and so on. See the suggestions under "Closing" for the letter M.

Or do the opposite: Organize a *running race*. Use the command *ready-set-go*. Students run from one side of the gym to the other.

Teaching Tips

- Remember to try out the music first before presenting it in class.
- Laminate signs and cues such as the red arrows and the valentine hearts so that you can save and reuse them.
- Students can help put red ribbons on their shoes by just pushing it under the shoelace. Tying knots isn't necessary.
- See "Stations" under the letter L for details about hanging objects in the tree.
- You can buy rocking boards or make them by putting a sturdy board with smooth edges over a block. For a greater challenge, use a sturdy piece of pipe that can roll (see figure R1).
- At the rolling station have a mat at the bottom of the incline mat. Check the students' technique; make sure they do not put pressure on the neck. See the gymnastics stations under the letter G, page 54 as well as the teaching tips listed there on page 55.
- At the running race there are no winners or losers; we are running because running is fun.

The Letter S

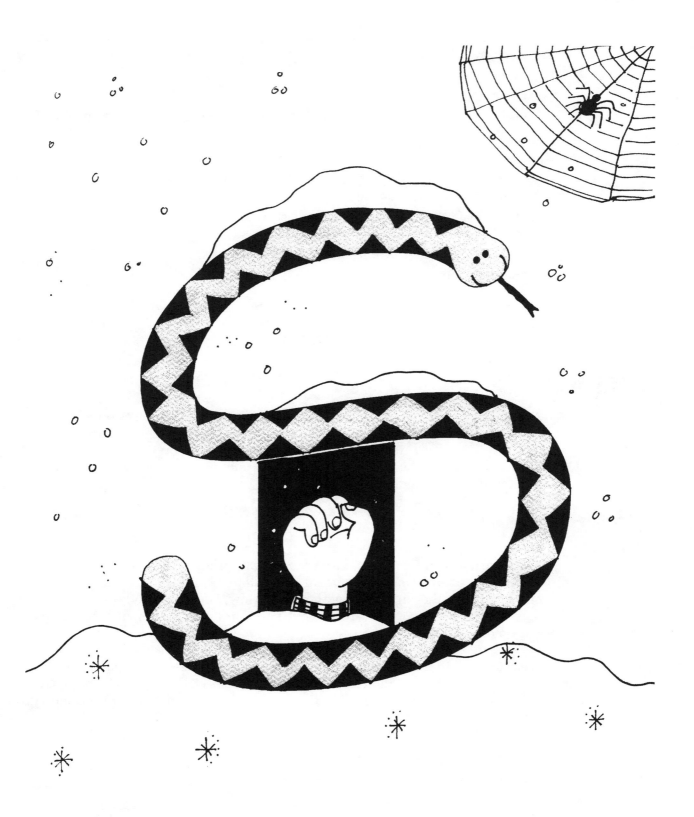

Words

Body parts: Shoulders

Nouns: Scarf, scooter board, shadow, snake, snowball, spider, square, stairs, steps, swan

Verbs: Sit, skip, slide, step, stretch

Direction: Sideways

Others: Shhhhh, six, seven, slow, start, stop, students' names that begin with S

Music

Aerobics music for step aerobics

Slow music or relaxation music for a scarf dance or shadow dance

Song: "Itsy-Bitsy Spider." Different versions are available. It is on the tape "It's Toddler Time" by KIMBO #0815. There is also a version by Little Richard.

"Sittercise" by KIMBO #2045

Song: "Swan" from "Animal Walks" by KIMBO #9107

Square dance music

Song: "Head, Shoulders, Knees, and Toes"

Warm-Up

As soon as the students enter ask them to "*Shhhhh!*"—be as quiet as possible, and repeat this throughout the lesson. Assign ways to move during the warm-up: *slide*, *skip*, take giant *steps*, move *sideways*, move *slowly*, and so on.

Have cutouts of the letter S available for students whose names begin with S and those who want or need to count laps.

Opening

There are many possibilities; the letter S usually takes a few weeks.

Design a *Scarf* **Dance**. Movement suggestions: Hold the scarf in one hand; move it in front, then in back; move it high and low; move it around your body and your legs; throw it in the air and catch it; use your other hand, switch hands. Try this on relaxation or slow music.

Perform a *Shadow* **Dance** by using a light source, such as the overhead projector or a flashlight and a large white sheet (see figure S1). Have students follow the movements and take turns behind the sheet. You can add Simon Says to this activity. The person behind the sheet is Simon. In addition, you can play relaxation or slow music.

"The Swan" and "Sittercise" have the movements spoken on the tapes.

"The Swan" goes as follows:

This is the *swan*, kneel on the ground

Sit back on your heels, body tall and straight

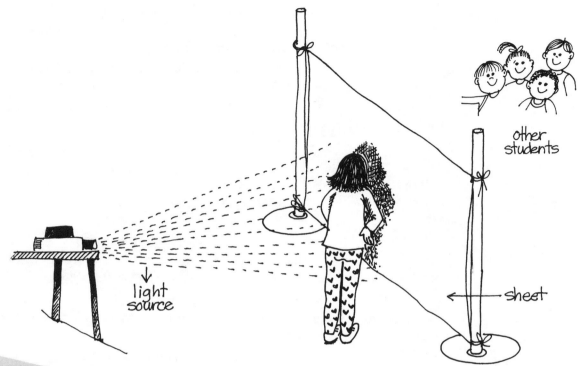

Figure S1   Shadow dance.

Pull back, arms front, reach front, arms back [repeat once]

Lie down on your stomach, arms *stretched* out front

Now lift, down, lift, down, lift, down

Pull back, sit on your heels

Arms stretched out front on the ground

Sit up, begin again.

Design a step aerobics routine. Use movements such as step up, step down, step over, step off to the side, and the like

The "Itsy-Bitsy Spider" song lends itself very well to adding movements. It is a lot of fun when you give each student a glove to wear, especially a black one. This gloved hand becomes the *spider*. Add extra movements such as spider on your head (put the gloved hand on your head), spider on your leg, on your foot, on your neighbor's arm, and so on.

How about a *square* dance? See "Opening" under the letter D for suggestions.

Song: "Head, Shoulders, Knees, and Toes." Emphasize that the word *shoulders* starts with an S.

Introduce the letter by having the students sign and verbalize the letter. Recognize words and students' names that start with S.

 Stations

Jump, climb, aerobics, push, dance, juggle, throw

- Tie one end of a long jump rope to a pole and move the other end back and forth over the floor as if it is a *snake*. Students try to jump or step over the rope.

- Jump to catch "snowflakes" that hang on a rope. The other end of the rope is attached to a doorframe, a beam, a hula hoop, or any other place using Velcro. Students jump up and pull them down.
- Climb up and down *steps* and *stairs*. Students can carry uppercase and lowercase letters with them and place in separate baskets.
- **Step Aerobics.** This works great as a station if you play a videotape of a simple routine. The students can follow the tape while you are assisting at another station.
- *Scooter board* activities:

  Students can push the scooter boards freely through an assigned space.

  They can kick a ball while on the scooter boards and keep the ball in the space.

  Students can follow a set path laid out by you as the teacher.

  Students can demonstrate how strong they are by pulling themselves along a rope hung between two volleyball standards (see figure S2).
- **Shadow Dance.** See under "Opening."
- **Scarf Juggling.** Challenge the students to juggle with two scarves at a time. Ask them to count to *six* and *seven*.
- *Snowball* **Fight**. This is always a favorite activity. Make snowballs from crumpled pieces of newspaper put in small plastic sandwich bags. Place a

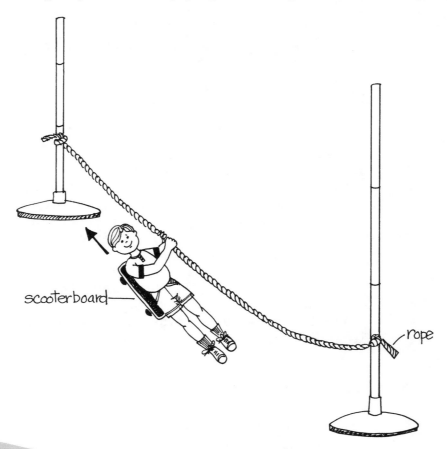

scooterboard

rope

Figure S2 Pull yourself along a rope on a scooter board.

divider between two groups. Each group has a laundry basket full of snowballs and keeps throwing them over the divider at the other group for a set time.

- Add any activities needed to meet individual objectives.

Play Area

The theme can be snow. Have hats and gloves available to make it more realistic. The snowball fight, jumping to catch snowflakes, and targets made of snowflakes can all go in the play area.

Closing

The snowball fight works well with the whole class if you have enough snowballs.

Play **Red Light, Green Light**. Emphasize *stop* for red and *start* for green. To play the game, all students line up on one side of the space. One player is It and stands on the opposite side of the space with back turned toward the rest of the class. When It says "Start," the other players move toward It. They try to get to It and touch him or her. When It says "Stop," all the players must stop. It turns around. If It sees anyone move, that player has to go back to the beginning and start over. Continue until a player makes it all the way and touches It without being caught moving. This player can become the new It.

Stretching is a great way to end a session. See the suggestions mentioned under "Closing" for the letter F on page 50 (flexibility).

Teaching Tips

- Ask parents for old scarves, order them from a catalog, or make them. Buy soft, transparent material at a fabric store and cut it into squares about 18 inches wide and long. Check with the store as to whether the material needs to be hemmed.

- If you do not have aerobic steps, use pieces of carpet and pretend they are steps by having the students step on and off them.

- A great project is to make your own step aerobics tape. Keep it simple, with only a few participants on the tape.

- Put mats under the steps and stairs used for climbing.

- At the shadow dance station, students can work in pairs. One student is behind the sheet and the other is in front. They switch places when a timer goes off, or talk about other ways of taking turns.

- For the snowball fight, the divider between the two groups can be as simple as a line on the floor. You can also use a net, gym mats turned on their sides, cardboard boxes, or tables.

- Snowflakes can be made by folding a square piece of paper in half at least two times. Use a pair of scissors to cut a pattern along the edges, then unfold the paper. Laminate the snowflakes for future use.

The Letter T

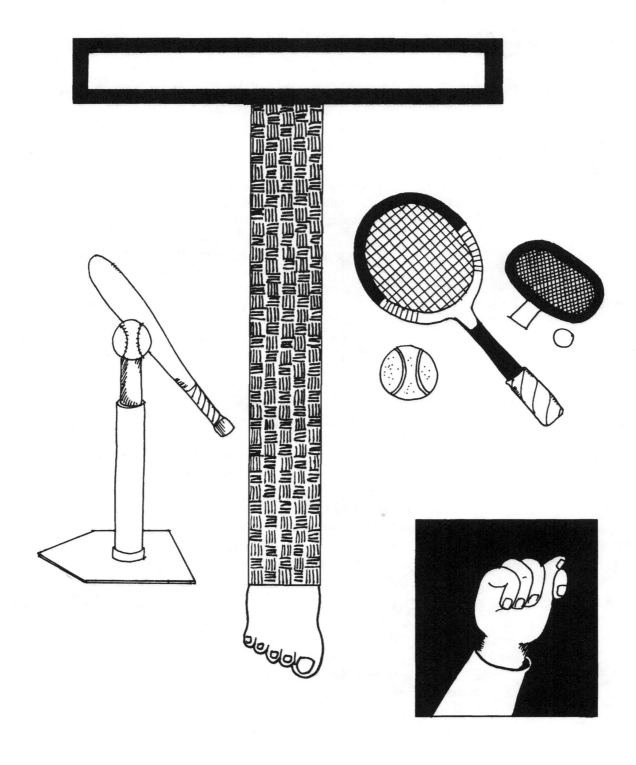

Words

Body parts: Toe, tongue

Nouns: Table, table tennis, tag, tail, tap, target, tennis, trampoline, tree, batting tee

Verbs: Tap, throw, toss, tumble, twist, turn

Others: Ten, three, tic-tac-toe, tiptoe, two, students' names that begin with T

 ## Music

Song: "Head, Shoulders, Knees, and Toes"

Song: "If All of the Raindrops Were Lemon Drops and Gumdrops"

Song: "Turning, Turning," sung to the tune of "Frère Jacques"

Sit-down rhyme

Aerobics music for tap dancing

Aerobics music for routine emphasizing toes

Rock 'n' roll music for doing the twist

 ## Warm-Up

Students walk or jog *three* laps. Designate parts of a lap where students need to walk on their *tiptoes*.

Have cutouts of the letter T available for students whose names start with T and those who need or want to count laps.

Opening

Students already are familiar with "Head, Shoulders, Knees, and Toes."

"If All of the Raindrops Were Lemon Drops and Gumdrops" has the following lyrics:

If all of the raindrops were lemon drops and gumdrops

Oh, what a rain it would be

I'd stand outside with my mouth open wide

Going ah ah ah ah ah ah ah ah ah [stick your *tongue* out]

If all of the raindrops were lemon drops and gumdrops

Oh, what a rain it would be.

The second verse replaces the line with "If all of the hailstones were Hershey bars and milkshakes."

The song "Turning, Turning" has the following lyrics:

Turning, turning

Turning, turning

To the left, to the right

I am getting dizzy

> I am getting dizzy
> Sitting down
> On the ground

The words for the sit-down rhyme are as follows:

> Touch your shoulders, touch your *toes*
> Reach up high and touch your nose
> Touch your head, touch your knees
> Cross your legs and sit down, please.

You can do the following with aerobics music or music selected for *tap* dancing. It works with and without taps on the students' shoes.

Invite the students to do the following:

Tap the left foot once, tap the right foot once.

Tap the left foot twice, tap the right foot twice.

Walk in place.

Jump up and down and turn around.

To create a routine emphasizing toes, combine the tap movements with the following:

Do a heel-toe with the left foot and with the right foot.

Walk on your toes, touch your toes, and so on.

You can also repeat the rock 'n' roll dance (the *twist*) from "Opening" for the letter D on page 37.

The students sign and verbalize the letter. Recognize words and students' names that start with T.

 **Stations**

Throw, toss, bat, strike, tumble, reach, jump

- *Tic-Tac-Toe* **Game.** Throw different-colored beanbags. You can play by the traditional rules (getting three beanbags of the same color in a row), or you can decide to count the number of beanbags on the game board when all the beanbags are thrown, or just throw at the target.
- *Table Tennis.* You can take the net down and put boards up on the side of the *table* so that the ball does not roll off. Give students a choice of paddle (table-tennis paddle or the larger wooden paddle) and ball (table-tennis ball or Wiffle ball) (see figure T1a).
- Bounce a *tennis ball* on a *tennis racket*. To prevent students from running after the balls all over the gym, use suspended balls or balls on a string attached to the racket. Count the number of bounces (see figure T1b).
- Hit a ball off a *batting tee*. Attach the ball to the tee with a piece of rope (see figure T1c).
- *Throw* and *toss* balls at *targets*. One of the targets can be a table turned on its side, and the balls will disappear behind the table (see figure B1 on page

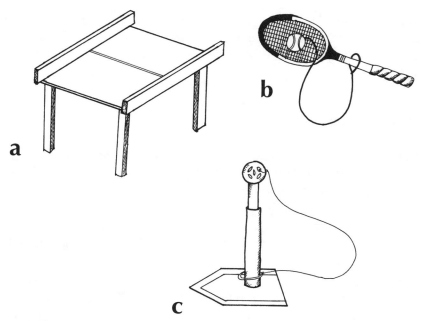

Figure T1 Batting ideas.
(a) Table-tennis table with boards on the side.
(b) Tennis racket with the ball restricted by a string.
(c) Batting tee with the ball restricted by a string.

28). Set up one station for distance throwing and another for precision tossing (for precision, the target is closer and the underhand toss is more successful). Half of the targets have the uppercase T written on them and the other half the lowercase t. Ask the students which one they are aiming for.

- *Tumbling.* Repeat the logroll, forward roll, and backward roll; demonstrate the donkey kick.
- Decorate the *tree.* Hang leaves (see the letter L) or hearts (letter R) in the tree.
- Add any activity needed to meet individual needs.

Play Area

The tumbling station is very suitable for this play area. You can expand it by adding other gymnastics activities, such as the balance/rocking boards and balance beams (see the letters A, G, and R); a *trampoline* to jump on; and a vaulting box to climb on and jump down from.

Closing

Catch the Tail. Each student gets a *tail* made from a piece of paper, ribbon, yarn, or the like. The tail is tucked into the back of the shorts. At least 10 inches must be visible. On the command "go," the students try to remove each other's tails while protecting their own. You can allow the students whose tails are gone to keep playing until all the tails have been removed. Who can get the most tails? Who can keep his or her tail the longest? Have the students hand all the tails to you, and then give them back to repeat the game.

You can also play a *tag* game. The simplest one is described under "Closing" for the letter D.

Teaching Tips

- Make a tic-tac-toe target from a piece of carpet or a gym mat. Tape or draw the pattern on the carpet or mat. You can also use floor tape to tape the tic-tac-toe diagram on the floor.

- Taps are available commercially, but you can make them from bottle caps attached to the soles of shoes with string and tape or an elastic band. Place the bottle cap under the ball of the foot with the ragged edge pointed toward the sole of the shoe, not the floor.

- Giving each student only one tap saves a lot of time and demonstrates the difference between the foot with the tap and the one without it.

- Students who cannot use their feet can put the tap on their hand.

- Adding a jingle bell to the Wiffle ball used for tennis and table tennis makes these activities very inviting. The bell also makes table tennis a great activity for students with visual impairments.

- Have the student bouncing a ball on a tennis racket stand in a hula hoop to emphasize control: hit softly, push the ball. Use rackets with short handles, or have the students hold the handle near the face of the racket (choke up on the handle).

- Use a regular table for the table-tennis setup since there is no net involved.

- A Wiffle ball is a great choice to start with. It rolls slower than a regular table-tennis ball and does not bounce much.

- Create more batting tees by using cones with a ball placed on top of each. Plastic bats are also recommended.

- For safety, put mats in the play area where needed—at the end of and under the balance beam, at the end of the incline mat, and behind the vaulting box.

- The Catch the Tail game sometimes benefits from being played in a smaller area.

- If a student is wearing a dress, attach the tail with a piece of cellophane tape.

The Letter U

Words

Nouns: U.S., umbrella

Directions: Up, under

Others: Students' names that begin with U

Music

Aerobics music

Music used for the step aerobics routine (see the letter S)

Warm-Up

Put barriers up for the students to go *under* (see figure U1). Barriers can be a rope between two poles, a rope over the top of two cones, the bars on the parallel bar, the balance beam, and the like. While doing their laps, students meet these barriers. Cutouts of the letter U are available for students whose names start with U and those who want to count their laps.

Opening

Repeat the step aerobics routine (see letter S, page 110), and mention stepping *up*. You can add other aerobic exercise–type movements: standing up (sitting down), jumping up, arms up, knees up, and so on.

The students sign and verbalize the letter. Recognize words and students' names that start with U.

Stations

Balance, push, climb, run

- Walk a star across the balance beam to a poster of the *U.S.* flag, and attach it (see under "Stations" for the letter A). If you use two flags, you can ask the students to distinguish between the uppercase U and the lowercase u. Write the letters on the stars and have the students place them on the correct flag.
- Students go under obstacles using a scooter board.
- Climb up on climbing equipment (sometimes referred to as whittle equipment) or vaulting boxes.
- Gather puzzle pieces of the U.S. and try to put them together. The pieces can be scattered all over the gym, or they have to be brought from one side to the other, one at a time, before everyone can make the puzzle.
- Add any activity to meet individual objectives.

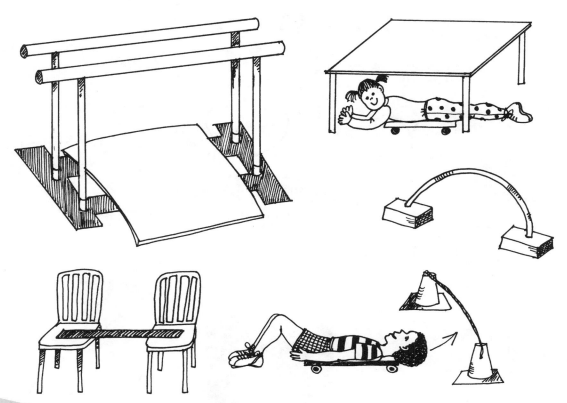

Figure U1 Obstacles to go under.

 ## Play Area

Offer a variety of obstacles to go under, using scooter boards as the means of transportation. Include the rope between two standards so that the students can pull themselves along the rope while lying on the scooter boards.

Closing

Have multiple puzzles of the U.S. available.

Organize a relay using the concept of under. Make tunnels from sheets draped over pieces of equipment and have the students go under them.

Teaching Tips

- Have mats behind the vaulting boxes and under the climbing equipment.
- Puzzles can be made out of large pieces of poster board that are laminated. This activity is easy to combine with a classroom geography lesson.
- On the balance beam, students can hold a pretend *umbrella*. Do not use a real umbrella because of the sharp points at the end.

The Letter V

 Words

Nouns: Valentine, vase, vegetables, vest, video, vitamins, volleyball
Others: Students' names that begin with V

 Music

Videotaped exercise routines

 Warm-Up

Start *videotaping* the lesson so that the students can watch themselves afterward in the classroom. Students walk or jog the warm-up laps. Have cutouts available for those students whose names start with V and those who want to count the laps.

 Opening

You can use a commercial exercise video, repeat a favorite aerobic activity, or have fun making your own. Either way, continue videotaping the lesson.

Discuss *vegetables* and *vitamins*. Show students examples. Then ask them to show you what the different vegetables and vitamins look like (shapes) and why they are good for us. For example: What does a carrot look like? (Stand tall, possibly with arms overhead.) Carrots are good for your eyes. What does a potato look like? (Roll up, but not too small.) Potatoes give you energy to jump. What does spinach look like? Spinach makes you strong. Vitamin C is in oranges; what does an orange look like? Vitamin C keeps you healthy.

Use this knowledge in a game of Simon Says. When Simon says "carrot," everyone takes on the shape of a carrot. When Simon Says "orange," everyone changes to an orange shape, and so on.

Verbalize and sign the letter. Recognize words and students' names that start with V.

 Stations

Walk, throw, catch

- **Clothing Relay.** Make *vests* out of newspapers.
- *Volleyball.* Use the same rules described for Newcombe (see under "Stations" for the letter N page 89, and figure V1).
- Hang valentine hearts in hula hoops and on strings as targets to throw at.
- Hang *valentine* hearts in the tree on the wall (see letter R, page 105). Half the hearts have an uppercase V on them and the other half a lowercase v. Ask the students to hang the uppercase hearts on one side of the tree and the lowercase hearts on the other. Or you can have two trees.

- Ask the students which of their favorite stations they would like to see videotaped.
- Add any stations needed to meet individual objectives.

Play Area

Select favorite stations, ones that you know the students enjoy seeing themselves do on videotape. Continue videotaping.

Figure V1 Volleyball ideas.

    (a) Regular volleyball setup with a low net.
    (b) Use of a divider.
    (c) Table as divider.
    (d) A rope between two chairs. Hang ribbons or scarves on the rope to increase visibility.

Closing

Pick Flowers. Scatter pictures of flowers and plastic flowers all over the floor, and ask the students to run and pick them up one at a time. Have a big *vase* ready for the flowers to go into. (A similar activity is discussed under "Closing" for the letter P, including a way to distinguish between uppercase and lowercase letters.)

Make a salad or a stew. Scatter pictures of vegetables, plastic vegetables, and maybe a few real potatoes all over the floor. Ask the students to run and pick them up one at a time. You hold a big bowl for the vegetables to go into.

When space and amount of equipment permit, the volleyball station can serve as an activity for the whole group. Use multiple nets and balls.

And, of course, continue videotaping.

Teaching Tips

- Whether you are just taping the lesson or making an exercise video, ask volunteers and parents to help videotape the lessons and donate the tape to the school.

- When making your own exercise video, plan ahead. Select the exercises you want to use as well as the music. What are you going to say at the beginning of the video? And for how long? Can a student do the introduction? Do you need to verbalize the exercises as they are being shown? Finish with a few simple stretches.

- If your school has a closed-circuit TV system, the exercise video can be shown every morning to get the day off to a good start. Select exercises that can be easily done in the classroom.

- One of the rules of Simon Says is that the students take on only those shapes that are preceded by the words "Simon says." If you do not say "Simon says spinach" but only "spinach," the students are not supposed to react. This requires good listening skills. You can choose whether you want to use this rule.

The Letter W

Words

Color: White

Nouns: Wall, warm-up, way, wheels, wind, window, winter, wonder

Verbs: Walk, waltz, wash, wave, whistle, wrestle, write

Directions: West, which way?

Others: We, western, students' names that begin with W

Music

Country-and-western music

Song: "The Wheels on the Bus" by Raffi, on the tape "Rise and Shine"from KIMBO #8111.

Song: "This Is the Way," to the tune of "The Wheels on the Bus."

Warm-Up

While country-and-*western* music is playing, the students *walk* their laps *White* arrows, lines, or yarn can direct the students. White cutouts of the letter W are available for those students whose names begin with W and those who want to count their laps.

Demonstrate swinging the arms to support the walk, and walk fast, slow, sideways, backward, on tiptoes, and so on.

You can organize the game **Which Way?** The students ask the question and you answer them, for example, north, east, south, or *west*. Post these four words (*wind* directions) on the four walls of your gym and have the students walk to the correct wall as fast as possible. The wind directions can be given in both uppercase and lowercase letters.

Opening

"The Wheels on the Bus" has the following lyrics:

The *wheels* on the bus go round and round, round and round, round and round

The wheels on the bus go round and round, all through the town. [make motion of the wheels]

Other verses:

The *windows* on the bus go up and down [move up and down]

The driver on the bus say move on back [lean back]

"This Is the Way" has the following lyrics:

This is the *way we* walk our feet, walk our feet, walk our feet

This is the way we walk our feet, all over town.

For other verses, replace the words "walk our feet" with "*wash* our face," "*wave* our hand," "*waltz* around," "*whistle* a tune," "*write* a note," and so on.

Do a country-and-western line dance set to the music. Use movements such as walking forward, walking back, heel-toe, kicking your leg, turning around, and clapping.

Verbalize and sign the letter. Recognize the letter words and students' names that start with W.

Stations

Throw, catch, wrestle, bat

- **Wall Ball.** Throw the ball against the *wall* and catch it. Each student can do this on their own or take turns with a partner. One person throws the ball against the wall and the other one tries to catch it.
- *Winter Wonderland 1:* Hang snowflakes or cutouts of snowmen for the students to throw at. Use white fleece balls or other white balls to represent snowballs.
- **Winter Wonderland 2:** Repeat the Snowball Fight (see "Stations" under the letter S on page 110 and figure W1).
- **Arm *Wrestling*.** Students can sit at a table or at a bench or lie on a mat on the floor.
- **Batting Station.** Suspend white balls, balloons, or bags. If using balloons, be alert. Use tennis rackets, badminton rackets, or hands to bat.
- Add any activity needed for individual needs.

Play Area

The activities related to snow make a great theme for the play area. Your Winter Wonderland can include the Snowball Fight, which children will play for as long as you let them. Have hats and mittens available for effect.

Closing

Play Which Way? again and use other words as well, such as "in the middle," "to the southwest corner," "diagonal," and the like. Post the wind directions in both uppercase and lowercase letters.

Teaching Tips

- For the line dance to be successful, practice at home first. Keep it very simple and do not expect perfection. There will probably not be a line. A scattered formation is very acceptable for this age group. The most important thing is to have fun.
- To give students more direction for wall ball, draw a line on the wall (students throw the ball above the line) and a line on the floor (students must stand behind the line when throwing the ball).

Figure W1 Winter Wonderland 2: A snowball fight.

- Counting how many times a student can catch the ball can be motivating. Can the ball bounce before it is caught?
- Notice the difference in success for wall ball between overhand throw and underhand toss.
- Arm wrestling can become too serious; keep it light by wrestling some students yourself.

The Letter X

 Words

Noun: Xylophone, Xmas (Christmas)
Others: Crossroads, pathways, shapes, students' names that begin with X

Music

Play the xylophone.
Aerobics tapes

Warm-Up

Two lines of students walk across the gym diagonally from both sides of the gym, crossing in the middle and thus forming the shape of the letter X. Instead of crossing in the middle, the students can do a high five and turn back to their side of the gym (see figure X1).

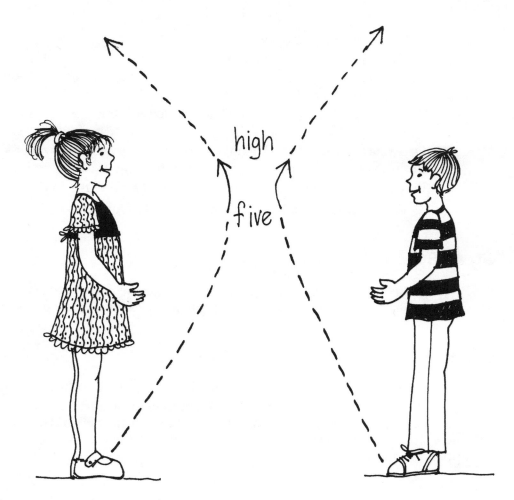

Figure X1 Walking a figure X from two sides, with a high five in the middle.

You can also a do basic warm-up of walking or jogging laps while you play a rhythm on the *xylophone*. Have cutouts of the letter X available for students whose names begin with X or those who want to count laps.

Opening

Mark each student's spot with an X instead of the usual carpet square or poly spot. Use a familiar aerobics tape from a previous lesson, such as "Aerobics USA," and play X Shapes. Ask the students which body parts they can cross to form the letter X. Some examples are arms, legs, fingers, and arm and leg, among others. Try to do aerobics with body parts crossed or include the motion of crossing in the routine. For example, instead of kick-and-kick and kick-and-kick, turn it into kick-and-cross and kick-and-cross. Instead of arms up, arms down, use arms out, arms crossed, arms out, arms crossed.

Sign and verbalize the letter. Recognize words and students' names that start with X.

Stations

Balance, throw, reach, run, play music

- Build your balance beams in the shape of the letter X. While traveling across the balance beams, students can carry uppercase and lowercase letters to be put in the correct basket.
- **Tic-Tac-Toe.** Play as described under the letter T, but use the symbols of Xs and Os instead.
- Decorate a tree. Each student takes one ornament at a time, walks across or through an obstacle course, and reaches to hang the ornament in a tree.
- Play on xylophones. While some students play, others can dance.
- Add any activity needed to practice individual objectives.

Play Area

Playing music and dancing are great activities for the play area. Have enough instruments available, including the xylophone, to keep all students busy.

Closing

You can repeat the warm-up of two lines crossing in the middle of the gym. Or organize a run where all the students hang ornaments in a tree one at a time and clean them up one at a time. If ornaments and a tree are not allowed in your school due to the implicit reference to Christmas, you can turn it into a run using the uppercase and lowercase letters.

 Teaching Tips

- Ask your supervisor or principal if you can use a Christmas *(Xmas)* tree. Some places will not allow this.
- Make your own tic-tac-toe game board by painting the board on a piece of carpet, or tape it on the floor. Mark the beanbags used for throwing with an O or an X.
- The tree can be drawn on a large piece of paper posted on the wall, and instead of ornaments you can have markers available for students to draw ornaments. If you do have ornaments, put a piece of Velcro on them and have Velcro strips on the tree.

The Letter Y

 **Words**

Color: Yellow

Nouns: Yard(stick), yarn, yo-yo

Others: "I love you," which is signed using the combination of I, L, and Y, students' names that begin with Y

 Music

Song: "Y.M.C.A." by the Village People. Also on the CD "Christy Lane's Complete Party Dance Music." See Resource B.

 Warm-Up

Use *yellow* arrows to direct the students or make a pathway using yellow *yarn*. Have cutouts of the letter available for those students whose names start with Y or those who want to count laps.

 Opening

Just about everyone is familiar with this fun song in which you form the shapes of the letters Y, M, C, and A during the chorus. Add movements as you see fit. You can repeat the line dance steps learned in the letter W lesson. Of course, you can always let the students come up with their own dance and dictate only the YMCA part.

Point out yellow on our clothes. Sign and verbalize the letter and recognize words and students' names that start with Y.

 Stations

Jump, run, yo-yo, bat

- Standing Long Jump. Measure the jumps with a *yardstick*.
- Running Long Jump. Again, measure the jumps with a yardstick.
- *Yo-yos.* Adjust the length of the string where needed.
- High Jump. Touch the wall at the highest point or touch a rope hung between two poles at its highest point. Slant the rope so that it is higher on one end and lower on the other. You can tape a yardstick on the wall for measuring purposes.
- Include a station where students measure their own height.
- Batting. Use yellow balls, beanbags, bags, or balloons. Be alert when using balloons due to the choking hazard.
- Add any activity needed to meet individual objectives.

 ## Play Area

Activities suitable for the play area are yo-yos and the batting station. Be careful when allowing the students to use rackets for batting.

 ## Closing

Teach (repeat) the sign for Y, and the sign for "I love you" (see figure L2, page 80). Repeat the warm-up exercise of following the yellow arrows and assign different locomotor skills.

Play a tag game called **Alien From Mars**. All students stand on one end of the gym behind a line where they are safe. The tagger stands in the middle of the gym and says, "I am the man from Mars and I will chase you to the stars if you wear the color ...[says color]." All students wearing the color mentioned have to try to cross the gym to the other side, behind a line where they are safe, without getting tagged. Of course, the color yellow has to be mentioned. You can change this by having the tagger show a big Y or a little y (uppercase or lowercase letter), and assign half the students to run when the little y is showing and the other half when the big Y is showing.

Teaching Tips

- Practice the opening routine with the appropriate music first before presenting it to the students.
- Create a standing long jump mat by taping a starting line for the student to stand behind. Perpendicular to the starting line, tape a line along which you can write the distance jumped.
- For the running long jump, you can use a line on the floor to jump from and a mat to land on. Be aware that the mat will slide along the floor with every consecutive jump and will need to be constantly adjusted.
- The string on a standard yo-yo is probably too long for young students and the yo-yo will hit the floor. Shorten the string or have the students stand on a platform.

The Letter Z

 **Words**

Nouns: Zebra, zoo
Others: Zigzag, students' names that begin with Z

 **Music**

The animals from the tape "Animal Walks" by KIMBO #9107
Aerobics music

 **Warm-Up**

Use arrows to lead the students in a *zigzag* pattern around the stations if needed. You can also use cones to mark the zigzag path (see figure Z1).

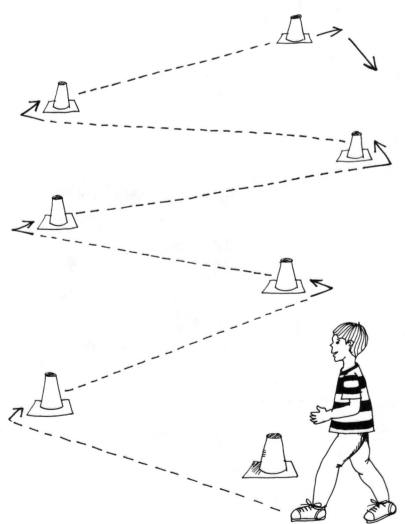

Figure Z1 Running a zigzag pattern.

Have cutouts of the letter available for students whose names start with Z.

Opening

The tape "Animal Walks" has the movements spoken on the tape. Most of the songs have been used throughout these lessons.

Ask the students to demonstrate how certain animals that are found in a *zoo* move. You can play the aerobics music in the background. Mention the *zebra,* of course. There are also lions, giraffes, monkeys, snakes, fish, elephants, and many others.

The students sign and verbalize the letter. Recognize words and students' names that start with Z.

Stations

Swing, crawl, push, juggle, balance, jump

- Swing on the ropes like a monkey.
- Slither through a tunnel like a snake.
- Lie prone on a scooter board for the turtle race.
- **Juggle Like a Seal.** Hold a ball on your flat hand, on the back of your neck, and on your head.
- **Get a Treat.** Walk across the balance beam with an ice cream cone with a ball in it.
- Jump on the vaulting box like a lion.
- Set up a drawing station. One large sheet of paper has the lowercase z drawn on it many times and another sheet has the uppercase Z. Ask students to draw animals using the shape of the letter.
- Add any stations needed to meet individual needs.

Play Area

Using the zoo as a theme, this is a great place to put some of the stations just described. Turn it into a circuit formation where students go from one station to the next in an assigned order (see figure Z2).

Closing

Repeat the zigzag from the warm-up or the animal moves from the opening.

Teaching Tips

- Put mats under the ropes, beneath and at the end of the balance beam, and behind the vaulting box.

- Make tunnels from large cardboard boxes or barrels. Or you can drape sheets over the backs of chairs.
- The turtle track can follow a set path. When it is part of the play area a circular path works well; students go around one time, leave the scooter board where they found it, and go on to the next activity in the play area.
- To decorate the play area use posters, stuffed animals, carpet squares to make a walkway, and a welcome sign (see figure Z2).

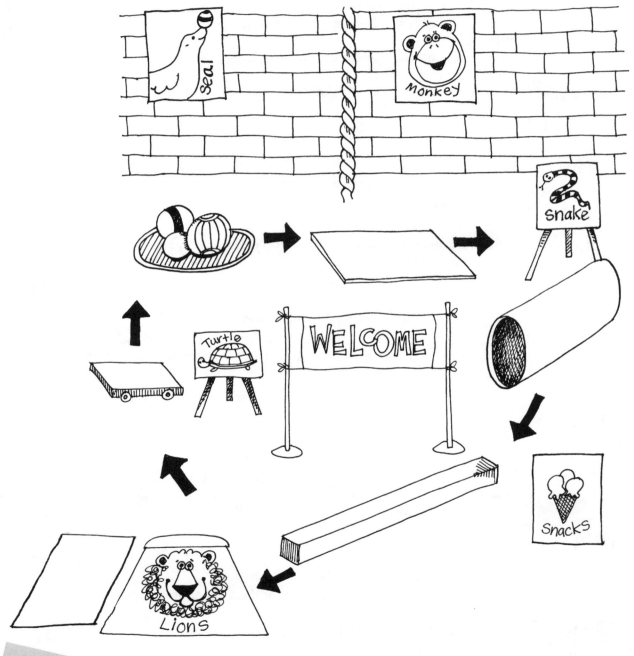

Figure Z2 Welcome to the Zoo. The seal balances balls, the monkey swings on the rope, the snake slithers through the tunnel, walk an ice-cream treat across the balance beam, the lion jumps on the box, and the turtle follows a circuit.

PART III

Resources

The following information is for you to use as a resource to save you time and increase your knowledge base. Resource A, "Activities in Other Support Areas," will help you create a multidisciplinary team. It provides you with ideas you can pass on to your colleagues in music, art, and media. The ideas are alphabetized. This resource is also useful to those of you who provide guidance to young children in more areas than only motor development. If you also have to design activities that involve more music, art, or media, this resource will be of great help. Resource A, together with the activities in this book, provides an extended curriculum.

Resource B, "Music and Songs," is an alphabetized list of all the songs and music mentioned in the book. Following each listing are the letters for which the song or music is used. This makes it easy to find the song or music in the book.

The parent handouts in Resource C are for you to copy as much as you need to. I recommend using your school's letterhead, drawing borders, cutting out pictures, or trying in any other way to make these handouts stand out when they are sent home. There is a handout introducing the program to the parents, a handout with a blueprint you can fill out to keep parents informed throughout the school year, and handouts related to specific letters. These letters are A, E, J, P, T, and Y. These handouts help to make health and fitness a family affair. Resource D provides names and addresses of companies, publications, and organizations where you can find even more music and activities or expand the activities mentioned in this book. Most publications listed here will help generate ideas when working with students with disabilities.

Resource A

Activities in Other Support Areas

Music

Compiled by Jane Huber, music teacher at Metro School in Charlotte, North Carolina.
The following suggestions are in addition to the listing at each letter.

- A: *If I Had an Apple* (to the tune of *If I Had a Hammer*)
- B: *Baby Beluga* (Raffi)
- C: *Take Me Riding in the Car* (Silver Burdett)
- D: *Little Puppy Dog* (Silver Burdett)
  Steady As the Beating Drum (Pocahontas)
- E: *One Elephant Went Out to Play* (Sharon, Lois, and Bram)
- F: *Won't You Be My Friend?* (Hap Palmer)
  Five Green and Speckled Frogs (Raffi)
- H: *If You're Happy* (Traditional)
- I: *Indian Play the Drum* (Silver Burdett)
- J: *Jelly in My Belly* (Sharon, Lois, and Bram)
- K: *Who's That Tapping at My Window, Who's That Knocking at My Door?* (Silver Burdett)
  Five Kites (Silver Burdett)
- L: *This Little Light of Mine* (Traditional)
- O: *Going Over the Sea* (Sharon, Lois, and Bram)
- P: *Pick a Bale of Cotton* (Raffi)
- Q: *Five Little Ducks* (Raffi)
- R: *The World Is a Rainbow* (Greg and Steve)
- S: *You'll Sing a Song* (Raffi)
  Splish Splash (Jim Valley)
- T: *Five Fat Turkeys* (Silver Burdett)
- U: *Going Over, Going Under* (Sharon, Lois, and Bram)
- V: *Will You Be My Valentine?* (Silver Burdett)
- W: *Willoughby, Walloughby, Woo* (Raffi)
- Y: *Yellow Submarine* (Beatles)
  I Love You (Barney)

Media Center

Compiled by Debbie Conrad, media specialist at Metro School in Charlotte, North Carolina.
Various media were used to introduce the letters to the students. Cooking, stories, finger plays with puppets, songs, videos, and arts and crafts were all used as teaching avenues.

Examples:

A: Alligator puppet.
  Making alligator cookies.
  Alligator hunt (similar to going on a bear hunt).

D: Cooking/making dog bones using peanut butter, dry milk, honey, and graham cracker crumbs.

E: One elephant went out to play (song by Sharon, Lois, and Bram). Student dramatization.

F: Make frog paper bag puppets.

G: Cooking gingerbread man.

M: Five little monkeys jumping on the bed. Finger play with puppets.

N: Make nifty noodle necklace using various sizes and styles of noodles.

P: Make paper plate pig.

Art

Compiled by Suzanne Tans, art teacher at Metro School in Charlotte, North Carolina.

A: Apple and seed prints on large block letter A.

B: Block prints.

C: Crayon drawing or coloring on crayon shape.

D: Dinosaur collage.

E: Cut paper elephant.

F: Fall leaf using real leaves pressed into clay.

G: Ghost wind sock.

H: Halloween pumpkin using stitching.

I: Ice cream colors.

J: Jeans using water color, cut paper, fabric.

K: Cut out and decorate kite.

L: Line collage or lamb using hand print and collage technique.

M: Merry Christmas ornaments.

N: Happy New Year or a hat collage.

O: Orange collage, paint with orange peels.

P: Painted penguin.

Q: Quilt.

R: Railroad of cut paper.

S: String butterfly, paint sunflower, make shakers.

T: Paint tulips and turtle mosaic.

U: Umbrella collage.

V: Indian vest.

W: Windmill with water color.

X: Collage in the shape of letter X using beans and rice.

Y: Valentine equivalents: I love you.

Z: (Zoo) animal masks.

Resource B
Music and Songs

Music

Country-western. See the country section of your local music store. The letter W.

"Electric Slide." On the CD "Christy Lane's Complete Party Dance Music." The letter A.

Halloween tunes, available at many stores in October. The letters G and H.

Lummi stick (rhythm stick) routine; KIMBO Educational has a variety of tapes. The letter L.

Marching band. On the CD "American Favorite Marches" by John Philip Sousa. The letter M.

From Jamaica. See the reggae section of your local music store. The letter J.

From Japan. Ask international clubs. The letter J.

Jazz. See the jazz section of your local music store. The letter J.

Limbo/Latin. The "Limbo Rock" is on the CD "Christy Lane's Complete Party Dance Music." The letters D and L.

Percussion. The music from the show *Stomp*. The letter P.

Relaxation. Ellipsis Arts (1999) has a collection of lullabies—Brazilian, African, and Latin. The letter R. Nature sounds can be relaxing also. The letter S.

Rock 'n' roll. "The Twist" on the CD "Christy Lane's Complete Party Dance Music." The letters D and T. Available through Human Kinetics.

Rock 'n' roll. Many stores have CDs available with greatest rock 'n' roll hits. The letter R.

Square dance. See your local music store or find a dance group in your area. The letters D, O, and S.

Songs

"Apples and Bananas" by Raffi, on the tape "Raffi in Concert," #KSR 0235 in the KIMBO catalog, has song lyrics on the tape. The letter B.

"My Foot Can Touch My Nose," to the tune of "The Farmer in the Dell." The letter F.

"Head, Shoulders, Knees, and Toes." The letters E, K, M, N, S, and T.

"Hokey-Pokey." Funky style on the CD "Christy Lane's Complete Party Dance Music." The letters H, I, L, O, and R.

"Turning, Turning," to the tune of "Frère Jacques." The letter T.

"If All of the Raindrops Were Lemon Drops and Gumdrops." The letter T.

"If You're Happy and You Know It." The letter H.

"Itsy-Bitsy Spider." Different versions are available. It is on the KIMBO Educational tape "It's Toddler Time," #0815. There is also a great version by Little Richard. The letter S.

"Old McDonald Had a Farm." The letters B, D, and Q.

"The Wheels on the Bus" by Raffi, on the tape "Rise and Shine," #8111 in the KIMBO catalog. The letter W.

"This Is the Way," to the tune of "The Wheels on the Bus." The letters F, I, and W.

"Let's Jump Up and Down," to the tune of "The Farmer in the Dell." Letter E.

"YMCA." Song by the Village People. Also on the CD "Christy Lane's Complete Party Dance Music." The letter Y.

Tapes

"Aerobics USA," by KIMBO Educational #8065, has movement directions on the tape. The letters A and O.

"Animal Walks," by KIMBO Educational #9107, has movement directions on the tape. The letters A, B, C, E, F, G, K, O, P, R, S, and Z.

"Bananaphone," by Raffi, #KSR 11115 in the KIMBO catalog, has song lyrics. The letter B.

"Hand Jivin'," by Educational Activities Inc., has movement directions on the tape. The letters C, F, and P.

"Me and My Beanbag," by KIMBO Educational #9111, has movement directions on the tape. The letters B and O.

"Nature Sounds," available at most record stores or nature stores. The letter I.

"Rock 'n' Roll Fitness Fun," by KIMBO Educational #9115, has movement directions on the tape. The letters A and C.

"Sittercise," by KIMBO Educational #2045, has movement directions on the tape. The letters F, J, and S.

Resource C

Handouts for Students to Take Home

Below are some instructions and hints on how to use the following pages of parent handouts.

Parent Handout 1
"Welcome" letter. Copy the text, replacing the date and other references with your school's name and policies. Use your school's letterhead.

Parent Handout 2
"Update" letter. Under Special Remarks write something positive and personal here about the specific child. This is also the place to mention a need for equipment and help. For example, you could state your need for newspapers or old socks. You can also remind parents of handouts you have sent home and ask them to please follow up with their child on these activities.

Parent Handout 3
"A is for the Air We Breathe." Repeat the poem a number of times in class so the student knows it when the handout goes home and can teach it to family members.

Parent Handout 4
"E is for Exercising." Part of our movement lessons and language stimulation program. Have a large copy of this handout in the classroom or gym and keep track of the exercises.

Parent Handout 5
"Let's Jump Rope." Part of our movement lessons and language stimulation program. Have ropes available for checkout to encourage students and parents exercising together.

Parent Handout 6
"Shake, Rattle, and Roll." Part of our movement lessons and language stimulation program. Share this activity with your art teacher also. Ask students to bring their homemade percussion instruments to school and use them in your lesson.

Parent Handout 7
"Terrific T-Songs." Teach these rhythms to the children just before sending the handout home.

Parent Handout 8
"How Long is a Yard?" Part of our movement lessons and language stimulation program. Send this handout home after you have taught the students to read a yardstick in class.

Date _____

Dear Parents and Guardians,

Welcome to Our School for the school year 2000-2001! We hope you had a fun and active summer. We are looking forward to the new school year and to working with your child(ren).

The movement activity lessons at Our School are nontraditional. Our program is a language stimulation program. The activities offered are an integral part of the curriculum, and daily activity sessions take place. Our goal is to teach the development of skills in a variety of areas such as physical fitness, rhythm and dance, gymnastics, and games. We are addressing literacy components along with the development of the skill areas. The components integrated in our activity sessions are letters, numbers, and word recognition as well as concepts such as colors, shapes, directions, body parts, and movements.

We believe young children learn best by doing. We offer this opportunity through our lessons and thus support the development of movement skills, language development, and cognitive development in an integrated setting.

The overall theme we are using is the alphabet. Throughout the school year you will receive updates on the letters being discussed, with a list of the words, concepts, and activities covered. Besides these updates, you will also periodically receive handouts describing small projects or activities you can do at home as a family.

When it is necessary for your child to miss a lesson, he or she must have a note from home. A child who must miss several consecutive days of class needs to have a doctor's note. Please refer to the Parents Handbook. Whenever possible, we would like for your child to participate to some extent and will work with you and your child to find alternative ways to participate. Your child can still benefit from the lesson even when not always actively participating.

For your child's safety, please send athletic shoes to school. Shoes with laces are preferred; sandals, flip-flops, slip-ons, clogs, and the like endanger your child when working in the gym or outside.

If you have any concerns or questions about our program, please feel free to call. Or come and visit us during the school day. Our door is always open. Thank you for your cooperation, and we are looking forward to a great year.

Mrs. Healthy
(111) 222-3333, ext. 44

Mr. Fun
(111) 222-3333, ext. 45

From *Movement ABCs* by Jolanda G. Hengstman, 2001, Champaign, IL: Human Kinetics.

Dear Parents and Guardians,

We are having great fun with our language stimulation program and are learning lots of words, movements, colors, and shapes, and much more.

The following is an overview:

The letter ___, and the words_____

The letter ___, and the words _____

The letter ___, and the words _____

The letter ___, and the words _____

Activities related to these letters and words are:

For the letter ___:

For the letter ___:

For the letter ___:

For the letter ___:

Special remarks:

Thank you for your interest. Please feel free to visit us at any time; our door is always open.

Mrs. Healthy
Mr. Fun

From *Movement ABCs* by Jolanda G. Hengstman, 2001, Champaign, IL: Human Kinetics.

A Is for the Air We Breathe...
We Need Air... Clean Air Is the Best

Activity 1
Have your mom or dad count the seconds out loud while you hold your breath. For how many seconds can you hold your breath? Your body makes you want to breathe again. We need air; it keeps us alive.

Activity 2
Ask your mom or dad to show you the air filter in your house. See the dust and dirt on it? Dust and dirt are in the air. If you know someone who smokes, look at their fingers or their teeth. Are they really clean, or are they a bit dirty?

Do you want to have that dirt go into your body?

Activity 3
The following poem is by the American Lung Association.

If you want to make friends
Smoking is not the way
'cause it leaves your teeth yellow
or maybe even gray!

None of us will ever smoke,
Not even as a silly joke,
And we will do our best each day
To make those cigarettes go away!

From *Movement ABCs* by Jolanda G. Hengstman, 2001, Champaign, IL: Human Kinetics. Poem reprinted by permission from American Lung Association, 1997, *A No Smoking Coloring Book*, New York: American Lung Association.

E Is for Exercising... Oh, What Fun!

Attached is a 30-day calendar with an exercise for each day. Do the exercise with your family, and be healthy, happy, and fit for a lifetime.

From *Movement ABCs* by Jolanda G. Hengstman, 2001, Champaign, IL: Human Kinetics.

Let's Jump Rope

Parents, do you remember how much fun it was jumping rope as a child? We have started working on this skill in class, and here are some easy ways to jump rope together.

Activity 1

If you have a hula hoop, your child can show you how to jump through it (see example *a*).

Activity 2

Make sure the rope is at the proper length. Measure a rope by stepping on the middle of it and pulling the handles up toward your shoulders. The rope is long enough if the handles reach the armpits. A rope that is too long or too short is going to make learning this skill difficult. Coiled rope works well when making your own jump rope.

Activity 3: Jumps to Learn the Rhythm

Use a rope cut in half (use both halves), or hold both handles in one hand. Jump and turn as if you are jumping rope. Keep the elbows close to the body (see examples *b* and *c*).

Activity 4: Long Jump Rope Skills

Tie one end of the rope to a tree, a fence, or other object. Turn the other end slowly, and invite your child to run through without jumping. You can also practice jumping. Hold the rope still, have your child stand next to the rope where it touches the ground, and you start turning.

Remember: Just have fun. It is not going to be perfect; find something your child can do.

From *Movement ABCs* by Jolanda G. Hengstman, 2001, Champaign, IL: Human Kinetics.

Shake, Rattle, and Roll
(the letter P is for percussion)

We have been practicing different rhythms and have listened to different sounds and beats. This is great fun. Here are a few ways to make your own shakers and rattles at home.

1. Use an empty toilet paper or paper towel roll.

   Decorate it using colored paper, markers, crayons, or the like.

   Fill it with dry beans or rice.

   Tape a piece of sturdy paper or plastic over the ends.

   Ready! Have fun.

2. Instead of a paper roll, use an empty coffee can, cream cheese tub, soda bottle, or other container that comes with its own lid.

   Put dried beans, peas, or rice in the container.

   Ready!

3. Decorate two paper or plastic plates using paper, crayons, markers, and so on.

   Put beans, dried peas, or rice in one plate.

   Place the other plate upside-down on top of first plate.

   Glue, tape, or staple the plates together.

   Your shaker is ready!

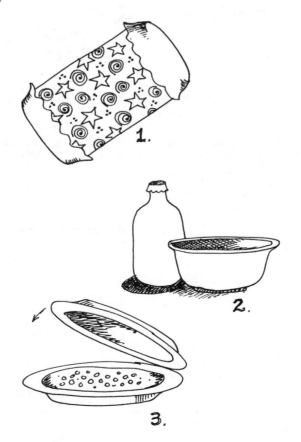

Terrific T Songs

Parents/guardians, ask your child about the following songs and rhythms if you have not heard them yet. We are having great fun with them. Here are the words so you can share in the fun.

1. The raindrop song (the T word is *tongue*.):

     If all of the raindrops were lemon drops and gumdrops
     Oh, what a rain it would be
     I'd stand outside with my mouth open wide
     Going ah ah ah ah ah ah ah ah ah ah ah ah ah (stick your tongue out)
     If all of the raindrops were lemon drops and gumdrops
     Oh, what a rain it would be.

   The second verse is, "If all of the hailstones were Hershey bars and milkshakes…"

2. "Turning, Turning," to the tune of Frère Jacques:

     Turning, turning
     Turning, turning
     To the left, to the right
     I am getting dizzy
     I am getting dizzy

3. Sit-Down Rhyme

     Touch your shoulders, touch your toes
     Reach up high and touch your nose
     Touch your head, touch your knees
     Cross your legs and sit down, please.

From *Movement ABCs* by Jolanda G. Hengstman, 2001, Champaign, IL: Human Kinetics.

How Long Is a Yard?

At school we measured different things using a yardstick. Let's see how long, wide, or high things are at home. Parents/guardians, can you help your child? If you do not have anything to measure with, use the ruler on the side of this paper. Use it to measure 36 inches of string or paper. This becomes your yardstick.

Object/Activity . . . Measurement

The front door is _____yards high.

Your bed is _____yards long.

You can reach _____yards high.

You can jump _____yards long.

An adult you know is _____yards tall.

A car is _____yards wide, _____yards high, and _____yards long.

From the street to the front door is _____yards long.

The living room is _____yards wide.

The window is almost _____yards high.

You are more than _____yards tall.

A coffee table is less than _____yards high.

One big step is almost _____yards long.

Guess how high the house is. The house is _____yards high.

Guess how high a tree is. The tree is _____yards high.

From *Movement ABCs* by Jolanda G. Hengstman, 2001, Champaign, IL: Human Kinetics.

Resource D

Suggested Readings and Resources

Music and Activities

KIMBO Educational
P.O. Box 477
Long Branch, NJ 07740
   (800) 631-2187 (U.S. only)
   Outside the continental U.S., call 732-229-4949
www.kimboed.com

Educational Activities Inc.
P.O. Box 392
Freeport, NY 11520
   800-645-3739 (U.S. only)
www.edact.com

Christy Lane's dance tapes, compact discs, and videos
Human Kinetics
P.O. Box 5076
Champaign, IL 61825-5076
   800-747-4457 (U.S. only)
   08 8277 1555 (Australia)
   800-465-7301 (Canada)
   09-523-3462 (New Zealand)
   +44 (0) 113 278 1708 (United Kingdom)
www.christylane.com
www.humankinetics.com

Jump rope guru Mark "Rock" Rothstein
P.O. Box 29654
Atlanta, GA 30359

Other Suggestions

Follow popular children's programs on TV for ideas
Broadway show tunes such as "Fame"
Dance Mix USA, distributed by Warlock Records Inc.
Internet

Publications

American Association for Active Lifestyles and Fitness, and National Association for Sport and Physical Education. 1995. *Including students with disabilities in physical education.* A position statement. Reston, VA: American Alliance for Health, Physical Education, Recreation and Dance.

Bornstein, H., and K. Saulnier. 1986. *Signed English: A basic guide.* New York: Crown.

Hammett, C.T. 1992. *Movement activities for early childhood.* Champaign, IL: Human Kinetics. (This book has additional resources and a list of equipment companies.)

Lieberman, L.J., and J.F. Cowart. 1996. *Games for people with sensory impairments.* Champaign, IL: Human Kinetics. (Contains resources for recreation and sport as well as an equipment resource list.)

National Association for Sport and Physical Education. 1990. *Developmentally appropriate physical education practices for children.* A position statement. Reston, VA: American Alliance for Health, Physical Education, Recreation and Dance.

Organizations

American Heart Association, Schoolsite Task Force
National headquarters: 7272 Greenville Ave.
Dallas, TX 75231
To obtain information about the Schoolsite Task Force, call (800) AHA-USA1 or (800) 242-8721 and ask for the phone number of the local office nearest you. Or check out the Web site **www. americanheart.org**
Offers Heartpower kits for students in kindergarten through eighth grade. The kits contain teacher resources, activity sheets, books, posters, and ideas on how to get everyone involved.

American Lung Association (or your local office)
(800) LUNG-USA
(800) 586-4872
The association has posters, coloring books, and handouts available.

Local international clubs; colleagues, friends, and families with diverse backgrounds.
Invite them to share traditional music, dance, and games. These are great opportunities for integrated curriculum by adding social, cultural, and geographical aspects.

references

Connor-Kuntz, F.J., and G.M. Dummer. 1996. Teaching across the curriculum: Language-enriched physical education for preschool children. *Adapted Physical Activity Quarterly* 13(3): 302–15.

McCall, R.M., and D.H. Craft. 2000. *Moving With a Purpose: Developing Programs for Preschoolers of All Abilities*. Champaign, IL: Human Kinetics.

National Association for Sport and Physical Education. 1994. *Developmentally appropriate practice in movement programs for young children ages 3-5*. Reston, VA: American Alliance for Health, Physical Education, Recreation and Dance.

Sanders, S. 1996. Preschool is different. *Teaching Elementary Physical Education* 7(6): 3, 9.

Werner, P. 1996. Interdisciplinary programming: An idea whose time has come again. *Teaching Elementary Physical Education* 7(4): 28–30.

about the author

Jolanda G. Hengstman is a physical educator at Sedgefield Elementary School in Charlotte, North Carolina. From 1992 to 1999, she was an adapted physical educator and athletic director at Metro School in Charlotte, a public school for students with developmental disabilities. Her physical education program was awarded the distinction of Demonstration School for Physical Education by the Governor's Council for Physical Fitness and Health and the North Carolina Department of Public Instruction. She also received the Governor's Council for Physical Fitness and Health's Youth Fitness Award for her efforts in 1998 and 1999. Hengstman is a Special Olympics coach and instructor for both aquatics and adapted aquatics. She earned master's degrees in adapted physical education from East Carolina University at Greenville and in physical education from the Academy for Physical Education at Arnhem, Netherlands.

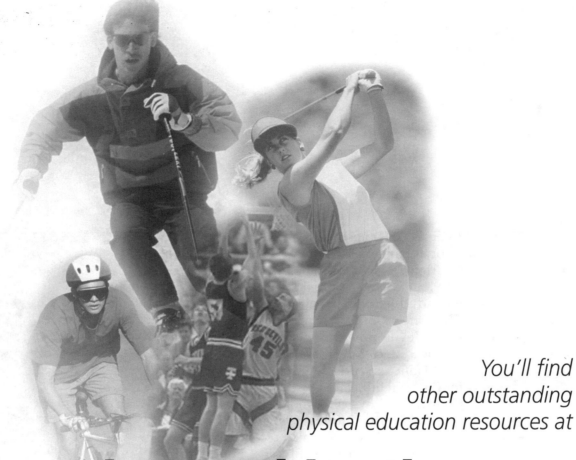

*You'll find
other outstanding
physical education resources at*

www.humankinetics.com

In the U.S. call

1-800-747-4457

Australia 08 8277 1555
Canada 1-800-465-7301
Europe .... +44 (0) 113 278 1708
New Zealand 09-523-3462

HUMAN KINETICS
The Information Leader in Physical Activity
P.O. Box 5076 • Champaign, IL 61825-5076 USA